Hope . . . From the Heart of Horses

Hope . . . From the Heart of Horses

How Horses Teach Us About
Presence, Strength, and Awareness

Kathy Pike
Foreword by Linda Kohanov

SKYHORSE PUBLISHING

Skyhorse Publishing books may be purchased in bulk at special discounts for sales promotion, corporate gifts, fund-raising, or educational purposes. Special editions can also be created to specifications. For details, contact the Special Sales Department, Skyhorse Publishing, 555 Eighth Avenue, Suite 903, New York, NY 10018 or info@skyhorsepublishing.com.

www.skyhorsepublishing.com

10 9 8 7 6 5 4 3 2 1

Library of Congress Cataloging-in-Publication Data
Pike, Kathy.
Hope--from the heart of horses : how horses teach us about presence, strength, and awareness / Kathy Pike ; foreword by Linda Kohanov.
p. cm.
ISBN 978-1-60239-660-9
1. Horses--Behavior. 2. Human-animal relationships. 3. Horses--Psychological aspects. I. Title.
SF281.P55 2009
636.1--dc22
2008055260
Printed in China

This book is dedicated to Flashy Doc Warrior, a.k.a. Moon.

The depth of his soul has brought me back to my own.
My first horse, he is always in my heart.

Contents

Acknowledgments

I extend deep gratitude to all of the individuals who have extended their trust to study with me; your courage gives others strength. Those of you who have allowed me to tell your story humble me.

Many horses have touched my heart and have provided deep learning for my clients: Hope, Amigo, Harley, Flash, Junta and Argentina, Sunshine, Mandy, Poppy, Ace, Annie, Africa, Pearl, Hannah Lei, Stone, Fly, Paint, Joy Boy, Beau, Gypsy, Patrick, and of course my boys, Moon and Corazon. I must also include Suki, my canine partner who taught me many life lessons.

Many thanks to all of the individuals at Skyhorse Publishing who helped to bring this manuscript to completion. Their confidence in this book and direction in editing was irreplaceable. The stories in the book moved from my heart to paper through Marty Humphrey's energizing coaching; she kept me writing. Marilyn Schwader offered continual spiritual and writing support and she polished a winning book proposal.

During a weeklong retreat under the aspen trees of Colorado, Nancy Wilhelms's creative eye captured the cover photo. Nancy Peregrine, Roberta McGowan, Maureen Luikart, and several other talented photographers have generously supported this and many other projects.

I honor Linda Kohanov for being a wonderful teacher and a pioneer in the area of Equine Facilitated Learning. I thank my colleagues who give their time and support to me: Karen Head, Isabelle Shock, and Terri Fisher. Mari Rubens, Alejandra Lara, and Dawn Calahan are dedicated students who have also supported the individuals and horses in my programs.

My spiritual sister Barbara Novak has witnessed my growth over the last twenty-five years. Her support has been a blessing. I express deep gratitude to John Baker for his contributions with the manuscript and photos, but most of all for his continual patience, unconditional love, generosity, and faith in me.

Foreword

The vast majority of centaurs were a rowdy, drunken bunch until Chiron came along. Resisting the bawdy temptations associated with his kind, the legendary man-horse tapped the ingredients of true genius, creating a maverick fusion of humanity and nature, intellect and intuition, strength and vulnerability, passion and reason all trotting around in one graceful, fleet-footed, four-legged body. Perhaps more important, Chiron's dynamic myth revealed a template for healing that transmuted difficulties into gifts and traumas into sources of power.

A celebrated teacher of heroes, Jason and Achilles among them, he not only strengthened his students' bodies and sharpened their minds, he instructed them in the soulful art of discovering their destiny. Yet Chiron's own path was altered by a seemingly senseless accident: during archery practice, he was mistakenly shot in the knee with a poison arrow. Delirious and limping in agony, he retreated into an underground cave to repair a potentially fatal wound. In trying different remedies, the centaur created the healing arts and went on to teach these skills to Aesclepius, the Greek god of medicine. Thereafter, Chiron became known as the "wounded healer."

Few people have lived the trajectory of Chiron's myth as closely as Kathy Pike. Fewer still are lucid enough to write about this transformational journey with such honesty, insight, and skill. Yet the multidisciplinary genius needed to create a book of this quality was the prize she received at the end of a sometimes painful, ultimately inspiring series of events that essentially turned her into a centaur. Inside Kathy's heart beats the soul of a four-legged woman, and a succession of living, breathing horses helped her access that secret power.

Early entanglements with drugs and a later serious riding accident set Kathy on a path of self-healing. Along the way, she developed the courage and fortitude to share her hard-won wisdom with others: as an author, lecturer, coach, entrepreneur, and, most recently, as an innovative clinician in the fast-growing field of equine facilitated human development, where horses teach people valuable life skills.

Like Chiron, her holistic approach to education and healing blossomed into the urge to help others discover their destiny. Her unique style of coaching empowers people by exercising that same, seemingly paradoxical combination of qualities that have brought her increasing success in her own life. Spend any significant time with Kathy, and you'll encounter a strong-willed, tenacious, refreshingly honest person who can also be tender, thoughtful, compassionate, and vulnerable. In short, she has learned to balance head and heart, logic and intuition, ambition and reflection in the truest tradition of the mythical centaur himself.

As Kathy became ever sounder of body, mind, and spirit, she accessed the resources to move beyond the riding trauma that robbed her of one of her greatest loves a decade earlier. Then, and only then, did horses come back into her life. This book is the story of what it took to reconnect with a species that fully embodies what Kathy is now eminently qualified to teach. With help from a series of equine guides, Kathy brought the most profound aspect of the Chiron myth to fruition in her own life—she became a wounded healer capable of teaching other potential heroes how to follow their own destiny, tapping the creativity, vitality, and courage needed to wrestle the hidden gifts from life's many difficulties.

I'm honored to be one of those two-legged creatures who have shared her journey at times, witnessing the profound ways that horses changed her life, the ways that she returned the favor, and the innovative partnerships she now forms with these regal creatures to initiate other lucky humans in the "centaurian" arts.

And I'm thrilled to recommend this book as one of the finest narratives on what horses have to teach people about life, love, power, and connection as we release them from their roles as beasts of burden and allow them to reclaim their true destiny as teachers, healers, and companions worthy of the deepest affection and respect.

—Linda Kohanov

Author of *The Tao of Equus,*

Riding between the Worlds, and *Way of the Horse.*

Introduction

In writing *Hope* I was fueled by my desire to help people understand how horses heal, empower, and enhance the lives of humans. I also wanted *Hope* to inspire compassion for horses and all living creatures. Lama Surya Das said: "Our lack of compassion stems from our inability to see deeply into the nature of things." When I returned to work with horses after an accident in my twenties, I shifted my perspective from what I wanted horses to do *for* me, and began to see what horses were offering *to* me. I needed to *see* the nature of horses instead of asking them to fit into my world. Thus, my real journey with horses began.

Hope offers stories about how horses touch and alter people's lives. Horses are now recognized for their capacity to transport individuals both spiritually and emotionally to higher levels of awareness. Equine-based learning programs and handicapped-riding centers are being established all over the country. The rise in popularity of books focused on the relationship humans have with horses, and even dogs and cats, offers promise that animals are now being seen as sentient beings.

My natural inclination as a Life Coach is to inspire and lift individuals to embody what is possible for them and to ignite their courage to bring their gift into the world. Horses are my partners in teaching and coaching others to achieve this goal. As Antoine de Saint-Exupéry said, "If you want to build a ship, don't herd people together to collect wood and don't assign them tasks and work, but rather teach them to long for the endless immensity of the sea."

Watch the exuberance of a herd of horses sprinting boldly through a field, and you will connect with the energy that lies within you and is waiting to be ignited with your passion. The unleashed power and complete physical freedom exhibited by horses inspire people to find their own inner freedom and uncensored expression of self that is analogous to the "endless immensity of the sea." I seldom suggest that clients "collect wood" or "assign them tasks and work;" instead I strive to teach them to see the world through a horse's eyes and learn the horse's way. Through this experience, their longing is awakened. Then the tasks to build an authentic life, the pieces that bring their life calling to realization, or the "ship," flow with clarity and enthusiasm.

A desire for connection to self, nature, and others fills the heart when one sees horses grazing in harmony. Horses' need for social structure and their non-judgmental approach to relationships ignite potential for the human heart to be touched, opened, and altered. There are no coincidences in what one experiences with a horse, be it harmony, rebellion, cooperation, union, or disconnection—everything has meaning. The interactions we have with horses directly reflect how we approach our human-to-human world. Horses are the mirrors to our soul.

Watch an upper-level rider in any discipline, and you will find deep connection and understanding between horse and rider. Achieving union and feel while balancing leadership can be a complex task. Horses are sensitive animals that easily understand and assimilate the "whole being" approach to relationship. *Hope* shares stories of how riders blend and integrate such aspects of the mind, body, and spirit to create higher levels of harmony and an invisible connection with their horses.

Horses need, want, and demand to know the leader in all of their relationships. A horse asks, "Who shall lead, you or I?" Quick to read body language, emotional messages, and verbal communications, horses give you exactly what you ask and respond in the manner that you have asked. Individuals in positions of influence learn to refine their leadership skills through learning the way of the horse.

The book's title came from a horse named Hope that you will read about in Chapter Three. Hope in its purest form is not simply being optimistic or wishing well. Hope is a spiritual experience that is uplifting and compels a person forward, creating momentum toward improving a situation. Hope acknowledges that the human perspective is limited, that which is current is not the full potential of what is possible. It recognizes that things can be and will be better in the unknown and unseen future and that goodness prevails.

Everything in my life transpires from continual waves of hope that move through me and propel me forward during tough times. I innately know that there are higher levels of unconditional love and compassion to learn and that it is animals, and especially horses, that are my greatest teachers. Their hearts, which are five times larger than the human heart, support me unconditionally and give me strength. Horses continue to teach me deeper levels of self-awareness, trust in myself, and heart-based leadership. They challenge me to look at my greatest fears and lift my spirit to greater levels of joy.

After you read this book, I hope that you see and experience all animals as sentient beings and teachers for humans. I hope the horses and people in the stories shared in *Hope* touch your heart and intrigue you to create a deeper relationship with a horse, and all animals. May you have the fortune to experience hope from the heart of a horse.

"In riding a horse, we borrow freedom."

—Helen Thompson

Dragged

Plastic horses in dusty dirt . . . invisible lines for fences. I would make my horses travel far, from one imaginary ranch to the next, jumping boulders, crossing streams, guided by my hand on their backs as my knees pressed into the ground, stone impressions leaving bumps and ridges in my young skin. Endless hours and timeless days spent in the dreamtime of horses, a wild cowgirl in the West. I played it all out in the backyard sandbox in a small town in the state of Maine. By day my herd would work and play; at night they would sleep next to my bed.

Years passed, and I grew from age seven to twenty-seven, when my games in the sandbox became fond memories. I had made it to the West and was just beginning to reach for my dream of horses. Seeking my childhood fantasies, I had saved my money to take my first set of riding lessons. Finally, my dream was becoming a reality. Two weeks of lessons with a young, energetic horse had hooked me. My joy was interrupted when I went away for a two-week holiday in Maine to enjoy the cool, moist coastal air. I could not wait to return to my new four-legged friend.

Back from my trip, on a fine August day I headed to the barn in the mountains of Utah. On this day I was unlucky and lucky both at the same time. It was a thrill to be back in the saddle. After two weeks away, the smell of horses felt like home, the home of my heart. This was the day I was to learn to canter. The sun warmed the fine, buttery smooth leather of the English saddle. My horse was a gorgeous five-year-old, 16-hand Trakehner warmblood. He was big, young, dark, and stunning. No one had ridden him while I was away. My instructor told me he might be a bit spunkier than usual —something about not having been ridden and his diet having more energy-rich alfalfa than usual. At the time her words meant nothing to me.

A four-second segment of this lesson would become a pivotal point in my life. As often as I think time flies, at times it slows down, stands still, and elongates as senses become heightened, alive, and fully engaged in the moment. These moments become memories. In the future they emerge easily, in full detail. At times these memories enhance our life, and at other times they stunt our growth and block potential. Memories are significant moments that shape lives and define the character of a person.

It is easy for me to remember aspects of that lesson on the glorious, sleek, and shiny Trakehner. One moment the soft leather saddle absorbed my legs and seat; the next I was bouncing on the hard, hot ground. Hooves pounded the dirt, a few feet from my eyes. My foot was stuck in the stirrup; my head banged on the ground, my body yanked and tugged relentlessly as the horse dragged me, stretching every joint in my body. To this day twenty years later, I can still see those hooves so clearly. Their multicolored tan—sparked with silver shoes, dusty from the ground they pounded—inches from my face, my head, my arms, my chest. I remember choking on the dust, being flayed by the sprays of dirt; the commotion, the screeching horse, and my instructor yelling. I remember those few seconds passing in slow motion. Those four seconds felt like long minutes. My life slowed while the horse unleashed a frenzy of power, throwing me on the ground and then dragging me by his side.

My head, safely tucked away inside my helmet, slammed against the ground. Suddenly, I heard a voice speak in my mind—my voice: "What did she tell me to do if I ever got dragged?" Another voice, clear and direct, replied—her voice: "Roll on your belly." I rolled over. Once I was on my belly, my foot instantly slid out of the stirrup. Everything came to a stop. Splayed face down in the dirt, my body was limp and still. At first I was not sure I wanted to move, or that I could. What just happened? Where was I?

After stopping the horse, my instructor ran to my aid. Bending over me, she asked, "Can you move? Is anything broken?" Her voice lingered, skirting on the edges of my consciousness, seeming far away, even though she was kneeling next to me. Slowly, I rose, first to my knees, then to a crouch, then, with her help, slowly to my feet. My body shook, and everything hurt like hell.

I might have hurt less in a show or training arena filled with soft sandy footing. This area was only a fenced sagebrush field, with a slight slope, naturally worn down by hours of horses and riders walking, trotting, cantering, and pounding the earth flat and unforgiving.

Sporting injuries were not uncommon to me. Days spent mountain biking, rock climbing, river running, and backcountry skiing had not all passed without accidents and close calls. My life revolved around the adventure of exploring the wild of nature. Near misses, chance accidents, falls and tumbles—too many to count. But not one had felt like this.

An excited, rapid stream of apologies came from my instructor's mouth. She repeatedly told me her horse did not mean to do what he did. She told me that I needed to realize this, and I needed to pet him and reassure him. This was the last thing on my mind. It was all I could do to glance at this horse. I could not speak. My mind screamed, "What about me?! *The hell with the horse*! I don't care about the damn horse. I am freaked out; I'm in pain, and my body H U R T S!"

Once assured that I had no broken bones, my instructor shifted her attention to her young horse. He stood against the fence, as far away from us as possible, head low and eyes worried. She immediately moved to him and began to console him. Tender words and strokes to his neck kept him still and quiet. Removing the saddle that hung beneath the horse's belly, she undid the remaining buckles, clearly disappointed that the leather had been ripped and her saddle destroyed. It was her best saddle. She fetched another from the tack room nearby and then announced, "You will get back on the horse." If not, she told me, I would always be afraid of riding.

I stood immobilized, traumatized, and partially dissociated. I refused. There was no way I was going to get back on the horse.

The instructor tried in every way she knew to convince me how important it was that "we," the horse and I, move past the episode and end with a good experience. Again, I refused. Every single cell in my body screamed, "No way! Danger! Death! Pain! That horse will kill me." I simply wanted out. I wanted out of the arena, away from her, and away from *that* horse. Ten weeks of companionship were voided, nullified and non-existent.

Recognizing my resolve, my instructor shifted gears. If I refused to get on the horse that threw me, then I would have to get on another horse that had watched the whole mishap. She fetched her older Appaloosa and saddled him up. I dreaded getting on the Appaloosa, but I folded; I had no energy to argue and thought the quickest way to get away was to do what she wanted. As I walked sparks of pain shot through my joints; stiffness was already setting in. I felt every part of my body, and every part of it was in pain. I could not tell whether any one area was more painful than another. Everything ached as if I had been trampled as well as dragged.

She helped me climb into the saddle and onto the white horse with reddish brown spots. This older, usually docile horse swished his tail; it was probably a fly, but it mattered not to me. My mind went wild with fear, anticipating another thrashing. There I sat for no more than two seconds—two very long seconds. Tears wanted release. Unable to allow them to fall, instead I wore tight, pinched lips in a frozen face. My instructor asked me to begin to walk the horse. I refused. I climbed off, declared that was good enough, and walked to the small, dark old shed that was used as a tack room. Hands still slightly shaking, I hung the helmet, walked off the property, and never went back. My instructor stood with her horses, watching me leave. It was the end of the beginning of my budding career with horses. Ironically, just weeks earlier I had expressed an interest in competing.

The next two days my tender body lay flat in bed, the scrapes and cuts sticking to the sheets. I could not find any comfortable position. My joints felt stretched and bruised. Moving required me to tune out of my body, hold my breath, and swallow back any gasps, as they would only trigger more pain. I had no health insurance, so a visit to the doctor was out of the question. I figured my body was healthy, and it would heal in time.

I was lucky. I remember how I had begged my instructor to let me ride without a helmet. She refused. I survived. There is no doubt in my mind that I would not be alive today if I had not worn that helmet. For this, I am grateful to her.

How did my accident happen? Had we buckled the horse's saddle wrong? Had something been poking into his belly? Was he simply feeling young and hot after two weeks in the pasture? Was there something about me that made my horse simply want me off his back? There could be many other reasons and/or explanations.

What was the horse's name? What was the instructor's name? To this day I cannot remember either. However, I remember the instant we moved into the freedom of the canter. I remember the *horse's* power moving through my body, the wildness, the rhythm, and the enormity of it. I remember that immediately following that connection came the disconnection, the flight of my body in air, and the thud when it hit the ground. But most of all I remember the hooves next to my face . . . sharp, vivid, and slashing. And the way everything moved in slow motion. A memory locked into my body, trauma and fear packed into my subconsciousness.

When I left the barn I left my dream of horses and part of myself behind. It took twelve years before I returned to horses. But when I walked away from the barn that sunny afternoon, I did not leave everything behind. I tried, but I failed. My body would not let me forget everything. It held the memory of the ecstatic joy of that first canter, the taste of freedom followed by being thrown and dragged. Letting go into a powerful flow had resulted in a hard jolt and slam.

Would it ever be safe to let go into my joy again? Could I trust life? Could I ever feel that level of power and freedom and feel safe at the same time? For years it was not possible. Instead I became the victim: always waiting for something bad to happen, most often during something that was joyful. I could never fully embrace a sense of feeling safe in my body, safe in the world, and safe to be me, to be who I am. Fear lived just below my skin, haunting my potential and restricting my possibilities. I had no awareness of this, no consciousness of the effects of that accident, nor that the gift of it would emerge years later in my life.

No one escapes trauma. No one gets to live life without it. Those who tell you that they have had a normal and uneventful life are kidding themselves, masking the incidents that have most shaped their consciousness.

Trauma, small or big, is significant. It shapes beliefs and perceptions and controls a person's ability to live a fully empowered and healthy existence. The human body holds the memory of trauma even when our conscious mind does not. Sometimes we can access those memories, as in my situation. Other times the body dissociates from the experience as a means to survive. Our coping mechanism decides that if death is near, it might be best not to be present in the body; therefore no pain can be felt. The body censoring the mind is actually a wondrous coping power. The conscious brain has no say in the matter. It is simply about surviving on the most basic, primal level of existence.

Our conscious mind can make decisions about how we can undo such traumas, rising above them and becoming more empowered and evolved through that experience. Undoing the trauma of this accident was a beneficial experience for me. What once was something I wanted to forget became my path to self-realization, my path back to myself, and ultimately the gateway to the very exciting and rewarding work I would do with others. The moment of trauma, the memory of it, was a defining moment in my life, one that would take work to undo and redo, but on the other side of the work was a joyous reuniting with myself, my whole self, a self that had more richness and complexity to offer than if I hadn't had the courage to do the work required to get there.

Now, twenty years later, I am a Life Coach. I work with individuals to help them realize and actualize their deepest dreams and the purpose of their lives. When I am coaching my clients to higher levels of consciousness, to realizing that path they were born to live and stepping into their authenticity, I often invite them to look at the most difficult and most joyous times in their lives. They remember and look at the moments of trauma, the periods of darkness, and the times they would rather ignore and keep hidden in the dark. They remember the times of bliss and joy, the moments and days that were the best of their lives. These moments, the good and the difficult, shape these persons and give them the clues to their gifts, leading them back to their true selves.

Every incident in life gives us the opportunity for growth, for exploring our awareness, and for reshaping our perception of the world. These most difficult times provide the greatest moments of definition once we are willing to look at them, heal them, and reclaim a part of ourselves that we might have given up. Reclaiming the joyous times ignites the energy that makes us feel whole and alive.

After the accident, I willed my childhood obsession and fantasies to die. There was no desire to heal this event in my life. Horses no longer existed for me. I blocked their existence from my life. I doubted the force, the desire that had been neatly tucked away, pressing against the surface all of my life. Allowing myself to have what I wanted, what gave me joy, resulted in danger, injury, and getting slammed into the ground, with twelve hundred pounds of muscle, sinew, heart, breath, and power poised over my physical and emotional body. The walls of protection rose and formed around me.

Thankfully for me, the horses would not allow me to keep hiding. My past wounds would not go without healing. It was twelve long years before I allowed horses to come into my consciousness again. Slowly they began to appear, tugging on my heartstrings, stirring my fears, tempting me as I moved with great trepidation. I did not seek horses out. Rather, they found me.

"The love for a horse is just as complicated as the love
for another human being . . .

If you never love a horse, you will never understand."

—Unknown

Polo Ponies

A few years after being dragged by that horse, in search of a more meaningful life, I chose to leave Park City. I was jaded by the decadence of living in a resort community, and it was time to move on and find something else. The recreational drinking, the drugs, and the uncommitted lifestyle, a lifestyle that lacked any sense of responsibility to one's self or to others, no longer appealed to me. After twelve years of living there, it was hard to move out of my patterns with the friends I had. Our habits, our routines, and the things we always did together no longer fulfilled me. It was time to break away, to change my life and reinvent myself.

Boulder, Colorado, was a strong draw because it offered an alternative community. Having just become a massage therapist, I found a nice niche doing bodywork in a chiropractor's office. I loved contributing to others' well-being in this way. My work was enhanced by my studies in polarity therapy and manual lymph drainage technique and through developing my own yoga, meditation, and personal growth practices. Significant changes in my life began to emerge naturally. I shifted from an outdoor-adventure and party-oriented identity to a spiritual path, cleaning up my diet and my habits. Taking a hard look at my life, my relationship to myself, and what I wanted for my future became a primary focus for growth.

Knowing that my life would continue to be based on being of service to others, I searched for another outlet for these desires. In addition to bodywork, my interests flowed into the area of helping others improve their lives through increasing their self-awareness and recognizing their passions and gifts. A fairly new profession called "Life Coaching" caught my attention, and my life shifted from adventure and exploration to learning more and helping others.

It was fall, and I had landed a job as a caretaker on a property just outside of Boulder that included a herd of four polo ponies. The owner seemed nice and fair. His Argentine polo ponies were small, around 15 hands each, but strong, with a bit of wildness in them. They were young and had been in the United States a short period of time. Polo season had just ended, and they would be out to pasture for the winter. It would be my job to feed them and keep an eye on them. It did not completely register in my mind that I would be taking care of the ponies; my accident had drifted into my past, becoming something I need not face again.

The caretaker's job landed me on twenty beautiful acres, just enough room for a few horses, a sense of space, and the peacefulness of the countryside. Newly built, the main house had yellow siding and a wrap-around white porch. It was modest, yet had style. The position included living quarters above the garage. It was perfect. It was clean and quiet and the work exchange worked well for me.

The herd consisted of two black horses, one sorrel, and a bay. All were mares, all the same size, and it took me a good month to tell them apart and to remember their Spanish names: Mulatona, Argentina, Sebastian, and Junta. My job was to throw hay to them morning and night and to make sure their water trough was full. One of these ponies, Junta, was feisty and aggressive, always at the front of the pack, ready for her food. She was the one I trusted least. She had a way of looking at me with her head held high that felt defiant and confrontational.

My apartment above the garage gave me a bird's eye view of the herd. I watched them during the day as I worked from my desk. It gave me great joy to see them so close, but my fears still ran me. All winter long I danced around them, negotiating my place among them. On the cold nights, when I fed after dark, I would cross the pasture to reach the barn where the hay was stored. Part of me loved these nights, not just because it was cold and dark. I enjoyed the elements and relished the star-covered sky, still free of the well-lit streets and malls of the surrounding towns. I would choose to go out without a light as my eyes became accustomed to the dark nights.

However, a bit of tension would fill my body until I crossed the pasture and finished feeding the horses. Only then could I enjoy the night. It was easy to feel and sense where the herd was resting as I ducked under the wood rails of the fence. And they would be aware as soon as I had crossed from my turf to theirs. The soft rustling of their movements rang familiar in my ears, one, two, and then three of them beginning to walk. Then there would be four, eager for their meal, moving now from a walk to a trot, footfalls getting lighter, legs lifting higher. I would feel and hear their collective energy build. Then the hooves would shift from a pleasant and light trot to a determined movement, a thundering stampede on the frozen ground. The earth would tremble like a freight train screeching through town.

As the sound of their storming hooves grew louder, I would break into my own version of a two-legged gallop, fearful that if I did not outpace them, they would trample me. Could they see in the dark? And if they could, would they care enough to go around me? I ducked under the electric fence in the nick of time. Panting with fear, I gulped the dry mountain air as the cold burned the inside of my nose. The hungry herd stopped on a dime, inches from the fence, their nostrils flared, shooting hot steam into the freezing night. They danced in front of me with their heads held high. Standing and staring back at them, I took refuge in knowing that just a thin line of electricity was between us. I relaxed a little at the sound of the electric current buzzing in the wire, threatening to zap their hides; I knew it was enough to keep me safe.

Sometimes I would laugh, even lecture the horses about being a bit more polite around feeding time. Other times I was angry when I barely made it under the fence or my mixed-breed dog, my comfort and constant companion, Suki, would get too close to the herd. When successful with my run, tuck, and duck, I would sometimes gloat in the power I held as the keeper of the food. Clearly it was my own method of self-protection and defense as my heart pounded with fear around this powerful force of nature. I played this game with them during the first few months. The ponies were being ponies, and I, a fearful woman, wanted to connect with them but was too frightened to do so.

As time passed there were more nights that I would stand with the horses as they mellowed out with their meal. Their heads lowered to their hay piles on the ground, and I stood close by and watched, listening as they crunched and tossed hay. As they continuously searched the silence around us for potential threats, I followed the movements of their swiveling ears, which scanned for any signs of danger.

Usually I would hear Suki hunting in the snow pack, chasing rodents and squirrels and occasionally picking up the scent of a coyote. She was my canine friend and full of life. A mix of shepherd, collie, and heeler, nothing got past her awareness. She was a hunter and runner. When she wasn't chasing her Frisbee, she chased the wind, biting at leaves in the air and running down small creatures in the fields. There seemed to be no way to stop this primal, instinctive behavior. She was relentlessly full of energy, yet as tender with children as a new mother. Highly sensitive and alert, she was at my side twenty-four/seven. During those nights with the horses, the peace would become a frenzy of barking, Suki hot in pursuit of a wild playmate.

The night was as alive as the day, especially when the moon rose to fullness. Staring at the ponies, I knew that if I were to make it through this caretaking job, I would have to stop playing games and start dealing with my fear.

The ranch owner offered a few suggestions on how to feel safe and set my boundaries with the hungry ponies. When around them, I learned how to maintain my personal space by making my presence bigger and releasing thoughts and fears that they wanted to trample me. The small tack room in the barn had a few training whips. I chose the small one, just three feet long. I used the whip to gain a little authority. Simply holding it made me feel a bit better. I knew I could use it if I needed to, though in my heart I had no intention of ever striking any of the ponies. That was not the purpose of the whip. Instead the whip extended the length of my arm. Suddenly I was bigger. When I extended my arm outward from my waist and gently swirled the whip I instantly felt like I had more space around me. The horses, being sensitive to movement and energy, would respond right away if I gave a swish in front of me or by my side. They would either stop and maintain the length of the distance where the whip had swished, or they would back off slightly, respecting the distance defined by the whip.

Watching the horses closely, I began to learn their herd dynamics and to see how they communicated with each other. If one approached another that did not want to be bothered, she might swish her tail as a warning, saying, "I see you—keep your distance." If the first horse ignored the warning, the other would pin her ears; her body began to tense, communicating a little louder, "I don't like your behavior." If the intruder continued to ignore these signs, the aggravated horse might snake her head out as a warning. If necessary, she would whip it again with more speed and intention, her action promising a bite. There would always be a progression of messages, each one more defined and intentional. One simply needed to pay attention to them and heed the warning.

At mealtime, the more dominant horses lowered their heads and moved toward another mare already in the hay. The eating horse, yielding power, stepped out of the pile to find a new place to eat. Dominance was established. Having lived together, the four all knew where they belonged in the group. Mealtime was a time to be reminded.

As I watched the polo ponies, I became curious about herd dynamics. It made me wonder whether when a herd became more stable, or spent more time together without the interruption of new members, each member became more accepting of their rank in the herd.[1]

It was clear where I belonged in the pecking order. I was the new girl, and I found myself at the bottom of the order, the least respected. I was going to have to focus on being physically safe until I had them figured out. Then, and only then, would I learn and apply ways to creep ahead and earn respect. Little knowledge and a big ego would only get me hurt again. Watching, waiting, learning, and using my instincts would keep me safe and alert.

---

1 I have found only one reference that explores this concept. In Stephen Budiansky's book, *The World According to Horses: How they Run, See and Think* (Henry Holt and Company, LLC, NY, NY, 2000), he writes about researcher Joel Berger. Berger spent over five hundred hours observing wild horse herds in the Grand Canyon area.

Berger found that in the six months that he observed several different bands, there was little to no change in the rank order within the bands. It appeared that during the nine months that I knew the polo ponies, they followed this same pattern of behavior.

It wasn't long before my heart softened and my defenses began to fade. Being with the horses on the ground was a completely different experience from a focused riding lesson. The more I observed, the more the horses became unique, alive beings to admire and cherish instead of objects for personal pleasure. I began to understand them the more I watched them. Fearful thoughts were replaced with curiosity and kindness. I began to entertain the idea of what it would be like to be one of them, so that I could better understand their behaviors. The more I sought to understand, the more things softened between us. I no longer ran across the pasture at feed time; instead I walked at my own pace, keeping my space, and the horses began to walk patiently behind me. The whip was put back into the tack shed and pulled out only on the coldest of nights when the group became unruly and ornery, hungry from the day-long chill.

On warmer days, we would all hang out in the pasture together between feed times. Sometimes I would sit on a low-hanging cottonwood limb, resting peacefully and centering myself as I had learned in my yoga practice. Sensing and feeling into my body, deepening my breath, my whole being would become more relaxed and present in the moment. It was at these times that Junta would come to me. Standing close enough that I could smell her wild winter coat, yet not close enough for physical contact, we would listen to the birds and watch the grass blow in the wind. Distant sounds pricked her ears to alertness. She was completely sensitive to every change in her environment.

It also seemed that all the horses responded to me according to my thoughts and energy. They were most willing to allow me to be a part of the herd when I was relaxed, open, receptive, and stress-free. In that state of being, I was in harmony and naturally flowed into the harmony already existing within their herd.

My fearful state only aroused them, causing tension as they read my energy and body language and became concerned that there was something for them also to be scared about. But once I shifted my fear and brought myself back into my body in a relaxed state, the horses relaxed too.

One by one, each at different times, they approached me, offering friendship. We all grew more accustomed to each other's antics and personalities. Moving around them in the pasture, at times subtly asking them to move for me, became joyful and adventurous. Holding a flexible stick the size of a whip, I would walk behind them and gently but intentionally wave the stick near the ground, creating energy. They would move along. I would stand in their spot, where they had been grazing, knowing that I had asked for movement and gotten it. I could do this with all of the horses except Junta, who always held her ground and gave me a look that would back me off.

Soon the stick would disappear and I would play the same game with only my body position and the intention I held in my mind and thoughts. Each time my confidence grew; simultaneously the horses responded. Slowly, we began to form an understanding. In time the herd accepted me; though I never felt they fully respected me. I knew better than to make such an assumption.

Later that winter the ranch owner hosted a party and invited me. A few teenage girls wanted to meet the ponies. In the middle of the clear, star-studded night, the party ventured over the snow-covered lawn and out to the pasture. There were no ponies to be found. I had fed them earlier, and they were very content. The girls called to them, but there was no response. Ducking under the fence, without halter or food, I walked in the dark over to where they liked to sleep. There I found Argentina, the sorrel mare, lowest in the pecking order. Of all of the horses, I was most fond of her. She lay contently in the snow, protected by the barren, scrubby oak brush behind her. I stood about three feet away and whispered to her, "Come now, Argentina, there are happy and excited young girls that want to love on you." She responded by releasing a long deep breath, rising, and shaking, and then she followed me across the pasture to where the girls were excitedly waiting. I stood back and watched the girls, fearless and joyful, loving on this gentle and kind mare. My eyes hidden in the darkness were bright with tears as I recalled the thirteen-year-old girl deep within me who wanted to play and love horses. My heart opened to the potential of the connection between horses and humans. Argentina had followed me without a halter. As my fears about horses diminished, the feisty polo ponies were transforming into loving sentient beings before my eyes.

It was not until spring that the horses sank deeply and completely back into my heart and hooked me back into their world. They achieved this with one very significant, unexplainable behavior.

My heart thawed along with the winter snow; mornings began to break earlier. The leaves on the trees began to bud, and specks of green poked through the dormant land. I felt my own urge of aliveness and desire bubble up within me. My thoughts kept going back to memories of a former lover, one I had never really gotten over, whom I had not seen or spoken to for six years. He was my companion in Park City. We had spent weeks traveling and backpacking together. His dark hair and blue eyes melted me; his easy wit made me laugh. We made a good team. I longed for such a connection again, a warm companion and a sensual lover to fill me with contentment.

The days lengthened and filled with blooming tree buds and bustling birds. The burst of life only added more fuel to my inner fire. I picked up the phone and called the lover I longed for. He was not that surprised, as the moment I called him he was sorting through old pictures of our times together. One thing led to the next and a weekend together was planned. He would drive from Utah to the ranch in Colorado.

He found his way along the dark dirt roads and arrived late at night. His delay did not matter to either of us, as finally being together again was what we both wanted.

After a night of passion I ventured out into the crisp spring morning air to feed the herd. My feminine energy was alive, my heart was open, and I felt a lightness of my spirit that I had not felt for years. As I rounded the corner of the house, the herd had already started to move to me. They stood at the far wood rail, heads turned, ears pricked at my approach. After a few nickers they came prancing across the field to me, manes waving and tails held high. They were dancing with excitement, gathered in a line about ten feet in front of me.

Then suddenly they did something I had never seen them do. In unison all four horses rose onto their hind legs. Standing tall, all four whinnied and called, their front hooves kicking and pawing into the sky, necks and bodies stretched high. Each became a two-legged dancing horse. Together they were a chorus line. Again simultaneously, they dropped their front legs to the ground. Now on all fours, they proceeded to lower themselves onto the ground, then onto their backs, tossing and rolling back and forth with great vigor. Their synchronized performance ended as they all rolled to the side, got up, shook off the dust they had just collected, gave me a good stare, and sauntered slowly over toward the barn for their morning feed.

My mouth dropped open and my eyes were wide. What was that all about? I had to laugh. Were they acting out the exuberance I had shared with my lover? Could they pick up on what was happening behind the walls of the house? Were they recognizing that special union of two souls? Maybe they were simply happy to see me getting a little loving, reducing my stress, and relaxing. I will never know what caused these ponies to dance with such deliberate exactness that spring morning, but it was a profound experience for me.

Never again did they offer anything even close to the same behavior. In the moments of their dance, my belief in how deeply we are all connected became confirmed on the deepest of levels. These sentient beings had opened up to me that morning and had offered communication with me like never before; in me they saw or experienced something that was worth noting. They did not dance for each other nor were they playing with each other. They had come to me and had danced in front of me, deliberately. They were talking with me.

I never rode any of the Argentine polo ponies, nor did I want to. I knew my limits, and experiencing them on the ground was good enough for me. The herd of polo ponies cracked the ice that had been sealed over my heart. They had helped me surrender my agendas and return to the rhythm of nature. Through our interactions I moved through some of my fear and found some stillness in my body. They mirrored my every feeling, thought, and judgment. I was far from the courageous horsewoman I dreamed of being as a child, but no doubt a bridge had been built, and I no longer felt I needed to alienate them from my life. My love for horses had been reignited.

> *"There is nothing so well known as that we should not expect something for nothing—but we all do and call it Hope."*
>
> —Edgar Watson Howe (1853–1937)

Hope

It was the morning after September 11, 2001, fateful 9/11, and I had just arrived on the coast of Oregon. I had left Boulder intending to retreat for the winter, practice meditation, and write a book. My coaching work was computer-based and conducted over the phone, leaving me free to live where I wanted.

Waves caressed the Oregon shore. A whisper of a breeze brushed against my skin. The sky was as clear as azurite, cloudless and pure. The sun danced softly, sending tiny sparks and twinkles off each sea swell. The ocean was gentle and calm. It was a peaceful day, yet, like most of us, I was filled with inner turmoil.

Struggling to come to terms with the horrid events that had taken place the day before, I sat in the warm sand, attempting to find meaning in the thoughts I wrote on paper. Beside me, Suki sat with a faded yellow tennis ball in front of her, waiting for the next moment of play.

It should have been a peaceful, perfect early fall day, a day that floats like a dream, mellow and soft, including a long stroll along the edge of the water followed by a comforting meal. It should have been a day of rejuvenation and rejoicing in the beauty of the world and Mother Nature. Yet the perfect canvas was smeared by an invisible presence, a feeling of darkness, of shadow, and deep sorrow.

My solitude was interrupted by the distant and familiar sound of approaching hooves. A woman and horse came flying down the open stretch of beach. The sheen of sweat illuminated every muscle and accentuated the curves and power of her horse's brown hide. Beside her trailed a younger horse, staying close by. The three of them moved in unison, a herd of three. Bareback, with her hair flying, the athletic, petite woman never lost her seat on the back of her mare. The horse's tail lifted high and proud; they moved from trot to canter, smooth as the glassy ocean as they flew to the end of the strip. As they turned around and bounded back, the rhythm of their movement stirred my body into a deep longing.

Every aspect of this trio screamed *freedom*. Nothing was in their way, and nothing held them back. Their full expression of power, exuberance, and presence stole my heart. A pure resonance of understanding and desire shot through my very core. My hips matched their rhythm; my whole being longed to experience what I was watching. My body shouted at me to get up and meet them on their way down. Yet I could not move. I could not listen to my desires; inner struggles prevailed.

Past me they flew.

Disappointed at my missed opportunity, I looked down. Staring patiently up at me was my beloved Suki. I threw her ball, then gathered my belongings and headed home, feeling that there was no real way for me to move beyond the mixed emotions of the day. The only place to be was exactly where I was. Consumed with sorrow, yet drawn to the allure of freedom I saw in the dynamic trio, I struggled to accept the reality of the world's current events. My eyes scanned the beach for the rider and her horses. A deeper part of my spirit wanted to believe something other than reality. I wanted to believe that what had happened in New York was not possible and that, instead, only beauty and peace were possible in the world.

The trio had stopped far down the beach. Was it possible for me to catch them? Was it my fate to connect with this woman? Memories of the dancing polo ponies surfaced, pulling on my heartstrings. Horses were calling for me. The polo ponies had broken the ice around my heart. As I watched the rider, something strong stirred in my body. There was a yearning for the physical connection of riding, for the sense of freedom it might bring me. A piece of me knew that I was kidding myself if I had thought that I would not long to ride again. Did I dare follow the deepest longing in my heart? I decided if it were meant for me to meet this woman and her horses, she would still be at the end of the beach.

And she was. Her name was Tammy, and she had stopped to talk with a friend. Trusting my gut, I stopped to say hi. Little did I realize that this one action, this one moment of following my desire, would be the beginning.

Tammy sat on her horse, her hard body a testament to her dedication to riding regularly. Her shirt and jeans were faded and worn. Her hand, stained and dirty, reached down to shake mine. She was a natural horsewoman—no pretense, no posturing, just a down-to-earth woman who loved horses. I knew I was about to make a new friend.

Tammy and I connected nicely, and she invited me to her ranch to meet her horses. Later that week I drove the winding narrow road leading to her green sanctuary in the hills off the coast. Crossing a small bridge over a stream, I entered her world. Fenced in smooth wire, her spread provided ample pasture for five horses. Four Quarter Horses, a brown, a bay, and two sorrels, along with a small black pony, roamed the property.

The property was a sweet spot filled with berry bushes and lots of trees and scrubs. The main house, set against a hill, was sided with natural logged wood, with a stone walkway leading to the door. To the right was a new covered arena, the focal point of the property. Behind it sat the original homestead, jacked up on blocks. Although it looked out of place and forgotten, it served as the tack room and hay barn.

Tammy wore jeans and a flannel shirt, and her thick, light brownish-blonde hair hung straight and natural to her shoulders. Her green eyes were stern, her lips pencil thin and drawn. She pushed her hair back from her cheek. Her fingers were stained, with black dirt packed under her nails. She had been out with the horses all day.

As we stood talking, a few of the horses began to meander over to us. Excusing herself, Tammy headed to the tack room for halters. I watched with a mix of amusement and trepidation as three curious horses approached. One horse, a sorrel Quarter Horse mare, took the lead and headed straight for me. Her head low and her eyes soft, she moved into my space with soft directness. Unsure of what to do, I stood still and trusted the moment. Then in one graceful motion she placed her head against my chest. Her forehead burrowed into my heart, and my whole being softened with her tenderness. Then my mind began to race with thoughts and images of being dragged across an arena, head pounding on the ground, hooves beating next to my eyes. I did not know what to do or think about this horse's gentle approach. Even the polo ponies had not initially connected with me in this way. In the moment of her gentle suggestion, a part of this auburn red horse wrapped around my heart. Her spirit enveloped me and has stayed with me since.

Tammy walked back from the tack room. "That's Hope," she announced. "Hope needs someone to give her attention. She is a boarded horse, and her owner does not have time to spend with her. I have too many horses to keep up with. If you're interested, why don't you create a relationship with her?" She smiled at us.

My heart soared at the possibility. Hope's sorrel coat shimmered with gold, reds, and rusts; a small white diamond sat above her brow. She was beautiful, if a bit out of shape and a little overweight.

Soon after our introduction, I was working with Hope, thirteen years after I had been dragged. To have this horse and new friend in my life was a blessing. In addition, a local horse trainer helped me move through progressions of groundwork and round pen activities. We began by checking on Hope's sensitivity, moving the rope around her body, swinging it around the back of her neck, and then asking her to back up with body language. Eventually we moved into the round pen, where I practiced lungeing her without a halter so she was free to do as she pleased.

It wasn't long before I understood why my accident years ago had happened. As I worked with Hope on the ground, I began to understand a horse's psychology. The groundwork opened up many doors for me, revealing insights about how horses respond to human pressure and how important it is that our requests are clear, firm, and free of doubts.

Horses taught me more about myself as I learned more about them. It became clear that bringing people together with horses, actually employing the horse as a teacher, would be a powerful experience for my life-coaching clients. Horses naturally communicate and tell us our intentions, even the intentions we might be unaware of, the ones held in our unconscious. Hope kept me on my toes and helped me to own my personal power and to communicate more directly with her. When I did, we danced. When I didn't, she ignored me.

Hope was the keeper of my childlike exuberance. Each time I interacted with her, more of me began to surface. From being dragged years ago, my fear of being in the saddle shrouded me, creating an element of resistance in our work. Day by day, little by little, Hope transformed my fear into willingness, which became anticipation of riding again. There was something about Hope that made me willing to try again. With the guidance of the trainer and Tammy, one day I simply climbed into the saddle and began to ride. Hope and I bonded through the saddle. I felt like a little girl who finally had what she had always wanted: a horse to call her own that she belonged to.

I had long ago left my life of outdoor sports in Utah, where I pushed my body to the limit while striving for the place often referred to as "the zone." In the zone, everything becomes harmonious and in sync. In the zone, there is no time, only pure flow and connection. Skiing, biking, and climbing had all been sports that helped me to attain the zone. The last three years I had focused on writing and working, and the zone, on a physical level, was not a part of my life. Little did I realize how much my spirit wanted to re-experience the zone.

Hope brought back the zone. During clinics we would reach the zone together. When we moved, it was as if we were one. I was not a skilled rider, but Hope did not seem to care. Seldom would I give her instructions with my hands or feet. Instead, I would simply look at what someone else was doing and say to her, "Let's do that!" As soon as I said it and thought it, she would do it. "Let's trot;" "Go around to the left;" "Do what they are doing." Each time my silent whispers reached her; she would comply. It was if the images that I held in my head moved into her body. Together we traveled as one; I was immersed in a sense of freedom and the thrill of reaching the zone with a living creature, and she had her desire for attention fulfilled. Hope made me look good, and she increased my confidence.

My excitement overflowed, and I could hardly contain myself. Being the talker that I am, I soon convinced my friend Sherri to join us. "You must try it," I told her. "It is so much fun. I will share Hope with you so you can experience this." Little did I know how this offer and encouragement would backfire on me. Sherri did join us and did experience Hope. She came to adore her, too.

Tammy was trying to get Hope leased for the winter. I returned from my vacation in Maine to find that Hope had been leased out from under me by my alleged friend Sherri. I felt betrayed by both women. How could someone to whom I had introduced Hope take her out from under me? I was devastated but there was nothing I could do. Tammy's financial needs drove her decision. The compassionate side of me could understand what she did. Yet the lack of communication with me before Hope was leased hurt deeply.

Hope now came to me in my meditations. Without my calling her, she would appear, her face directly looking at me in my mind's eye; I could not ignore her presence. Never before had an animal come to me in this way, powerful and disturbing at the same time. She was calling for me, she wanted to be with me, yet her fate was out of my hands. Visions of her moved from pure ecstasy and connection to dread and the sense of failure. I had failed to take charge and create what I had wanted with this wonderful animal. During one meditation, I simply told her the truth and told her she needed to work with Sherri for now. After that, Hope's presence in my meditations diminished.

Devastated and disappointed, I made the choice to move from the coast of Oregon back to Colorado to return to my caretaking position with the polo ponies. At least I would be back in the sun. The herd had grown from four horses to sixteen, the ranch owner informed me when I asked for my old job back. I would have my hands full. It felt safer to move back and be with my trustworthy friends. But my heart was filled with sorrow. My connection with Hope had not been fully broken; in fact, it was still very present. Close to my heart she remained.

Just a few months later, Hope's face began to reappear in my mind's eye. I brushed off these experiences as coincidental. Then one day she was stubborn. For the life of me I could not get her name or her face out of my awareness. As I sat at the computer, she would emerge; driving my car, I saw her again. My tears flowed.

Finally I heeded the message and called Tammy. Tammy told me that just the day before, Hope's owner had experienced a family tragedy and could no longer keep Hope. Hope had been given to Tammy. Unfortunately, Tammy had no interest in this horse and did not want her. Sherri had bailed on her lease now that the harsher months of winter had rolled around. Hope was in limbo. Then Tammy returned to find Hope had cut her foot in the pasture. I had called that very night. Now Hope needed extra care.

Tammy and I began to talk about the possibility of my purchasing Hope. She knew we had a strong connection, and she knew I wanted to have her. Winter months rolled by as I tried to figure out the best way for me to make this life-changing move. Just as I had hesitated on the beach, I hesitated about the purchase. Could I really have what I'd always wanted? Could I successfully provide for this horse? My hesitation, doubt, and lack of confidence were further fueled by rational horse friends and fiscally responsible mentors who reminded me of how expensive and time-consuming a horse would be. My optimistic, spiritually based community ignited my hope and desire to own Hope. They encouraged me to follow my inner guidance and dreams. Indecision prevailed. I took no action during the winter months.

But that spring I found myself in my car driving back to the Northwest. I pulled into Tammy's rutted driveway. There she was, my girl Hope, bright as the spring grass, standing right next to the gate awaiting my arrival. How did she know I was coming? Through the gate I slipped to share warm hellos and silent greetings. We walked to the old house that served as the tack room. Out hopped Tammy. An afternoon of play felt like coming home to my dear four-legged friend.

During the following week Hope and I worked together, rediscovering our dance on the ground and then enjoying a bit of bareback riding. Tammy told me that it was obvious Hope and I belonged together. She told me she would not sell her before I was ready for her.

Three days later I arrived at the ranch, only to be told that Hope was gone. Tammy had traded her for a young brown-and-white pinto, an exciting new project for Tammy. Devastated, I left feeling betrayed yet again, and I questioned my own sense of commitment. If I had only acted on my desires, things would have turned out differently. What sort of insane person believes the word of someone who had already lied? But for me it was normal. I had always wanted to believe in people, a level of naïvete that did not serve me in life. No matter how many times a person would fail to keep their promises, I always wanted to believe that the next promise would be kept. Even though I made promises to myself, over and over, not to believe everything a person told me, my heart continually wanted to trust and to believe that a person could love me enough to keep their word with me. But here I was again, being shattered by promises broken, trusting those who were not trustworthy. Life happens, and people break agreements.

When does a wish for something interfere with receiving it? Mixed inner emotions and the lack of ability to own my power, to claim what I wanted—the life I wanted and the horse I wanted in it—kept me from creating it. Instead, I remained passive and hopeful that things would simply work out. Was I blind to the special bond that Hope and I shared? I think so, and it took me many years to find a horse I trusted as much as I did Hope. My ignorance and hesitation had cost me a dear companion.

Hope is still wrapped around my heart. As with a lover whose scent and sweet gestures linger on one's mind, all others rarely compare. There is no opening for another. Instead the constant feeling of desire for my connection with her remains within me. This is the feeling called hope: to desire something with confidence and fulfillment against all odds. Hope has a gentle feminine quality to it. To fulfill and have success, there must also be resolve and commitment. Hope is positive and focused on possibility. Yet a part of me struggles with the concept of hope. To hold hope in one's heart without other actions or intentions may leave too much room for other possibilities.

For years now I have carried the hope that Hope would come back to me. Sometimes I try to let it go, to send her away from my history, my memory, me. Other times I try to conjure up an image of her in my mind, pining for the special connection that lies between worlds, feeling the ease of our unity in my legs, hips, and body. I sense she is content, maybe grazing in the green grasses of the Oregon coast. I also sense that she is not fulfilled.

Hope helped me begin my path of healing through equine connections. She opened not only a door to my own healing, but also the door to the work that I would bring to the world. She put light in my mind and heart, teaching me about the powerful connection and learning that can happen between two beings who do not communicate the same way but, when allowed, can share a deeper level of communication, one that happens in the heart and soul. It feels unjust to me that she and I are not together. It feels unfair that the horse that so boldly picked me, who wanted me and continued to ask for me, is with someone else.

I remained without a horse to call my own for four more years. Part of me knew that another horse would eventually come to me. Another part of me wondered if I would continue to long for connection without finding it, just the way I had spent years looking for that one man to connect with yet I continued to feel constant betrayal or rejection from unfortunate circumstance.

Were my constant obsessive thoughts and hopes of having Hope shutting the door to creating a connection with another horse? Was the hope of having Hope enough?

"We are all travelers in the wilderness of the world, and the best that we can find in our travels is an honest friend."

—Robert Louis Stevenson

Amigo

In the fall of 2004 I had returned from Oregon. The caretaker's position at the polo ranch was filled, so I found myself living in a small condo in Boulder, Colorado. Volunteering for a local nonprofit organization that offered equine-based learning programs for disadvantaged children fulfilled my desire to be around horses. It was a good situation, with many horses from many diverse backgrounds. Some were donated and some were rescued. All of them were in need of attention and care. I enjoyed my time there, but I felt frustrated nevertheless. My heart still dreamed of having my own horse and working with people and horses to expand human awareness and growth.

To make a living, I continued to offer life-coaching services to individuals going through transitions or building their own businesses. All of the work I did was over the phone. I often worked with individuals who lived overseas and in Canada. When I was not working on the phone, I was working on my computer, writing newsletters and marketing myself over the Internet. This job gave me great flexibility and was highly rewarding, but it lacked personal contact. Sometimes I would spend up to three days by myself, Suki my only companion. During this period, my work went through a dramatic transition. Many of my clients had completed their work with me, and no new clients were coming in. Every day I sat alone at my computer launching programs and classes to my current client base. I had no replies. Nothing was happening; my programs were not filling. I was in a slump. What I really wanted was to be in the company of horses.

In the previous year I had sent two of my coaching clients who were also interested in being with horses off to other teachers for equine experiential learning sessions. One of them came back and told me she had signed me up for a weekend workshop in December at Linda Kohanov's ranch in Tucson, Arizona. When working with Hope I had read Linda's two books, *The Tao of Equus* and *Riding Between the Worlds*. Linda struck me as a brave pioneer in exploring the potential in human-horse relationships. Six months previously I had started to write an application letter to attend Linda's first apprenticeship program, but when I reviewed my bank account I could not see how I could make it happen. My coaching business was too fickle to support such an investment.

My client, the CEO of a company, had plenty of resources for this venture. She was seriously considering the apprenticeship program. I was excited to go to the clinic in Arizona with my client, but I also felt more than a little tentative about the experience. My heart wanted to step into the work, but my mind kept reminding me of my limitations. I was full of limiting thoughts: what-ifs, whys, maybes, maybe-nots, and hows. At that time I had no horse, no barn, and no real vision of what I wanted. All I knew was that I wanted to be with horses and humans in a learning environment and to bring that combination to my coaching clients. The volunteer work helped to fill my horse-time needs. I enjoyed mucking stalls and helping others with their programs. However, it did not provide an opportunity to grow and expand into being a teacher of equine-based learning programs.

Like the winter fog on the Oregon coast, depression settled onto my shoulders, wrapping me in discouraging words and punishing thoughts. My desires seemed so unattainable that I began to shut down. The deeper my spirits sank into depression, the darker my days became. Simultaneously, and as a result, my coaching business continued to evaporate. Even though I had little income to support a trip to Tucson, I made the decision to attend the program. It was easy to justify my actions by telling myself that it would help my depression and that I owed it to my client to support her in her passion and process in working with horses.

During my Arizona stay, I shared a home with three other women who were attending the workshop. Everyone was excited about what the workshop would bring us. We traveled together in a rental car along the dirt roads that led to Linda's ranch. The road was bumpy and hilly, crossing a few dry riverbeds. Finally the car rolled down a small hill to reach the ranch that sat in a quiet spot on the edge of Tucson.

The other three women talked nonstop; their frivolous chit-chatting started to irritate me. It had started as soon as we had gotten out of bed, and it appeared that it was not going to decrease throughout the weekend. No one was really listening to each other. Instead, they continually talked over and interrupted each other, their excitement spilling out uncontrollably. I couldn't wait to get out of the car.

Out of the car, I headed off by myself, striding to the beautiful white adobe house sheltered on one side by the hillside. In the front of the house were several penned areas and round pens, each with a single horse in it. The horses were busy eating their breakfasts. Each raised its head to look at me as I walked past toward the house. They instantly put me at ease.

The reprieve did not last long. There were over fifteen participants and ten women facilitating the workshop. I was amazed at the large number of participants and also at their willingness to share aspects of themselves that one only shares with the closest of friends. I sensed that a very emotional weekend was about to unfold. My body began to stiffen, and I felt the old familiar invisible curtain of self-defense falling down around me. Surely I could not fully participate in this workshop with my client as witness. That felt personally uncomfortable and professionally inappropriate.

I worried about what my client would think about me if I broke down emotionally, revealing my past. She, like me, had become an expert at taking refuge in her head, rationalizing choices and her life. Both of us were learning new ways to reconnect to our emotional selves; this workshop promised an unknown potential of what could transpire. This did not ignite my excitement. Instead, it sent me into my own sacred protective space, one that I had developed after years of giving emotional support to members of my family and receiving little in return. It was the only way I knew to survive when people started to dump their emotions around me, when they dropped into deep processes. I could be present for them, but only if I wore a tight band of self-protection and self-preservation around me. I was a master at giving to others but never letting anyone near my heart. Dread washed over me as I realized I was here for the whole weekend. The emotional sharing and processing irritated me and made me feel vulnerable. I feared my inability to contain myself within my private space and not feel everyone else's emotions. The only protection I knew was to keep my walls up. My secrets were better kept in the closet; I feared letting anyone see my weak spot, my vulnerability.

After meeting all of the women and going through introductions, we were finally invited to meet the horses. Stepping outside gave me some breathing room. The horses, known for their work with people, were all standing patiently waiting for us.

One horse caught my eye. His name was Amigo. He was a smaller horse and new to the ranch. No one knew what breed of horse he was. He was obviously a mix of breeds, but the best that anyone could do was a "best guess." With his shaggy hair and firm, strong body, he would have been cute, if it had not been for the look in his eyes. His brown eyes looked distant and glazed over. He looked so far away it was impossible to connect with him. He stood in his stall, mouth wrapped around the cold metal fencing. He pulled back his lips to show his big teeth moving back and forth along the rail, grinding and scraping, rhythmic and relentless. To me his whole body screamed of the desire to escape confinement—for freedom. Raising the hair on the back of my neck, it sent shivers down my spine and my body tightened. I found myself slightly repulsed by him.

We gathered into small groups and shared our experiences in meeting the horses. Then we were told about their histories. Amigo had an interesting background. Until the ranch, he had had no real home but traveled across the border between Mexico and Arizona. His former owners used him as a packhorse, an efficient delivery system for the illegal transport of drugs. They would load him up with drugs, give him a hard whack on his rump, and send him galloping by himself across the border. That was not a pretty life for a young horse. He was a means to an end, a tool for illegal activity, never cared for properly.

Later that day it was determined I would work with Amigo. At first I found it odd that I would be working with him. Of all the horses, he was the one I found the most undesirable. I did not really like him or feel drawn to him. However, he was the one I had the strongest reaction to. I decided to go with this strong response and to experience what this horse might teach me.

As I approached Amigo's pen, the memories I wanted to avoid came flooding back. At the age of nineteen I had left my home in Maine in search of a life, an adult life. I bought a one-way ticket to Phoenix, Arizona, hoping that there was some thing in the West for me.

Instead, I found myself hanging out with a group of people who enjoyed using recreational drugs. I was easily influenced to join them and soon found that much of my time was spent in unhealthy ways. We would stay up late at night indulging ourselves, only to rise the next day, work, and party again at night. Each day became one long blur. I spent my earnings from my job and then I tapped into and blew all of my savings. I became disconnected and irresponsible and did not care what was happening to my life. My self-esteem was in the gutter.

Finally, I missed a morning shift at work and was fired. Anger, shame, and hopelessness sank into me. I needed an out. Luck was on my side. A job opened at a resort in Wyoming. Counting my blessings, I packed my bags and bought another one-way ticket. A shuttle car picked me up at the airport to take to my destination. It was late May in a late spring. Two feet of snow still blanketed the ground, slushy and dirty. I wondered what I had gotten myself into. I knew for sure, whether I liked it or not, I was getting away from the bad influence of friends in Phoenix.

Healthier life choices became my focus while living in the mountains. I threw myself into outdoor activities, turning to hiking, biking, and mountain climbing to strengthen my mind and body. Still feeling like a loser, I pushed the edges of safety, tempting fate, feeling little value in my future.

All of these memories came flooding back to me as began to walk to Amigo, the horse assigned to me. Nerves on edge, I shared my past experiences with my facilitator, Charlie, the ones that occurred in that part of the desert countryside. Charlie was tall and lean; her well-weathered skin hinted of Native American bloodlines. Clear green eyes and a strong, compassionate voice complemented Charlie's bold physical presence. Gently she reminded me that not just my life savings had been taken from me during my days of using drugs, but my innocence and the youthful, joyful time of young adulthood. I had not thought of it in those terms. I reflected on that statement, recalling my friends' stories of their wonderful adventures in college, time spent learning and exploring adulthood. I, on the other hand, had destroyed a precious part of my life, the time for discovery, learning, and exploring. My innocent eyes and fresh perspective had disappeared. I had learned to view the world as harsh and unforgiving. I believed that what I had would always be taken away from me.

I had not thought about this part of my life in this way before. It seemed important to see it from Charlie's point of view, to recognize and mourn what I had lost, and to finally release the shame and guilt from my mind and my spirit. It was a profound insight and has remained with me to this day. It was serendipitous that I would return to Arizona and be matched with a horse with a drug-related history in order for these memories to resurface. I had not realized that I had packed away this memory to hide my weakness from others. In doing so I had filled myself with shame.

A session of grooming grounded me physically. Even as I groomed Amigo, I feared him. I did not trust him. I had been told he could be a bit nippy because he did not trust others. At best, I was tentative. I cut my time short, feeling safer watching the woman I was partnered with work with him. My emotions were stirred up, and I felt raw.

That night I woke at three A.M. Words from the deepest part of my subconscious poured out into my journal. I wrote without making much logical sense. I allowed my pen to flow and race along the paper that fast became stained with tears. Old anger moved through me as I wrote about those who influenced me. Grief rose as I realized all of the time and opportunity I had lost. I was still seeing life through the same low-self-esteem lenses.

Shame washed over me. How could I have wasted so much of my life and myself? How could I have been so financially irresponsible? My poor habits were short-lived, yet the magnitude of the effect on my life was not. Shame I had been carrying for years began to release from my spirit through my pen. Self-forgiveness replaced the anger. Lost pieces of me came back to my heart.

Trapped in the victim mentality, I was blind to how the past was influencing my present life. My abilities to realize financial security and to create meaningful, long-lasting career opportunities were limited. Amigo had opened up the memories and given me an opportunity for learning. I could let the past unconsciously run me for the rest of my life, or I could forgive myself and move on. The choice was mine, only mine.

In the morning I squeezed myself back into the car with the chatty group of ladies. I felt exhausted. Staring quietly out the window as we ventured back to the ranch for the second day of the workshop, I was thankful for all the chatting, which allowed me to become invisible.

The morning workshop involved every woman sharing her own honest emotions and processes. Not surprisingly, many of the women had experienced betrayal, self-deception, rejection, loss, and abandonment, all leading to long periods of lowered self-esteem and suffering. The ages, faces, and figures in the room were different, and the content of the stories was different. But we all shared similar personal and life challenges stemming from those life-altering events. We sat for two straight hours. My anger from the day before had softened, and I felt myself feeling more compassion for all of the other women who sat in the room, exposing themselves and finding the courage to move through their own traumas.

It was time to experience the horses in the round pen session. Our assignment was to enter the round pen with our chosen horse and to do whatever felt right for us. It was a pretty open-ended assignment. This type of structureless work can release a wave of fear in even the most confident individual.

Anne, the thin woman paired with me, was in her fifties, rather quiet and petite, strong in her body, and composed. She had an easy-going, open nature, and I was glad that I had a partner who was so experienced. Anne had her own barn at home and gave riding lessons. She was intrigued by Amigo's complexity and history and was drawn to work with him. Ironic, I thought, as I was still somewhat repulsed by him. Her session with Amigo began. Confidently she entered the round pen. After just a few minutes she reached up to stroke Amigo on his neck. Swiftly his head swung back at her. This gesture did not feel like he was inviting more touch. Instead it felt like a pointed response, almost a warning. It was quick and direct. His neck shot to the side and reached toward his mid-section, where she stood. Amigo's ears were pinned back, and his face was tense. He was giving clear signs: an unhappy horse communicating the desire for space.

Anne either missed the signal or ignored it; perhaps I was overly sensitive. She reached out, and once again his head swung back, but this time he snapped at her. He caught part of her hand. She pulled her hand back, grabbed and held it with her other hand. My body filled with fear. Amigo had snapped at a woman who had horse experience. Surely he would do more with me, the one shaking with fear, without any real experience.

Anne's session ended, and she shared her learning with the rest of the group. She explained that she was having challenges in keeping good boundaries at her barn. Recently she had taken on new boarders. Anne confessed to the group that often she aimed to please others in order to feel connected and liked, but she had failed to set solid boundaries with the new boarders in her barn. When she would see a boarder being unsafe with a horse she often would say nothing, in fear that the person would no longer like her. Then other times she was overly eager trying to help people. She lacked consistency in her boundaries. She feared that some of her boarders could cause physical harm to themselves while interacting with horses because of her poor example setting, both with people and horses. Amigo had given her a nip on her hand, to remind her of his boundary and the space he needed in their relationship, a space that she was completely unaware of. This helped her to see how she could be more aware of how she was asserting her energy and how her eagerness to please others and connect too soon could cause harm.

Squirming in my seat, my mind raced with fear. I waited with dread. Soon my facilitator, Jennifer, called me to the edge of the round pen. There she instructed me to take a few deep breaths and focus on my grounding.

Standing beside the round pen, I felt tremendous fear surge and pulse through every cell of my body. My legs were shaking so powerfully that I thought I would not be able to remain standing. I thought I might throw up. Every part of me wanted to run as fast as I could in the opposite direction. I wanted out! Yet another part of me wanted in; I wanted to have this experience. I wanted Amigo to teach me. I wanted to experience him. I also wanted the fear to leave my body. My desires overrode my fear, and, even though my body was rattled to the core, I stepped into the round pen.

Once in the pen, I again scanned my body for sensations in an effort to become congruent—meaning to be fully aware of what I was thinking and feeling and where I might be carrying stress in my body. Horses respond more positively to a person who is congruent, or honest about what is happening in their body and mind. In other words, horses prefer you are not hiding any agendas, intentions, or unconscious emotions such as sadness, anger, frustration, or fear. A person who projects one thought or intention but holds the opposite feeling in her body creates a confusing message for the horse.

Horses communicate through what they feel internally, on an instinctive level. The safety of the herd depends on each member's ability to sense danger from predatory animals. Predatory animals, including humans, hold stress in their bodies. This stress not only creates a different physical posture but a particular chemistry and smell. Horses are tuned into all of these levels of information and can easily identify another animal with predatory intentions. They sense when they need to move from danger; they sense when it is safe to graze. In a herd, horses communicate with each other through their feelings and reactions. When one horse becomes nervous and instinctively moves to safety, the whole herd moves together, as if they are sharing the same pool of knowing, of consciousness. Their communications are finely tuned, and messages transfer faster than the human mind can comprehend.

A human who is in an incongruent state of being—thinking one thought while feeling a different emotion, or carrying an agenda and trying to hide it—gives off the same vibration or stress signals as a predatory animal in the wild. A person who is trying to project happiness but is feeling anger or frustration will eventually find their horse becomes difficult and frustrated too. A person who is filled with fear but puts on a confident face may experience a horse who does not cooperate or respect them, or will not join up. Horses couldn't care less what you are trying to appear to be; horses sense what you *are* feeling, who you *are*, even if you are unaware of it yourself.

Intuitively I understood the importance of this fact and then everything and everyone around me fell away. I was only aware of Amigo and myself and the space inside the round pen area. Because being congruent was important to the herd dynamics of horses, once I entered the round pen, I entered into Amigo's herd. He already had trust issues, so I knew I could not lie to him and continue to be safe. After years of being a bodyworker and yoga practitioner and of practicing meditation and being aware of body sensations, I knew that I could communicate what was true for me. Amigo could do whatever he wanted with that information.

I entered the pen and remained about four feet away from Amigo. In my mind I told Amigo every sensation I was having and which areas were affected in my body. I kept focusing my awareness through my body, bringing my attention to the area that was most alive with fear and trepidation. In my mind I began to talk to Amigo. I told him that my legs were shaking and that I was extremely afraid, but I did not know why. I told him I was unsure if my feelings belonged to me or if they belonged to him or perhaps the people watching, but I felt them strongly. A person viewing us from the outside of the round pen might have assumed that little was transpiring. Amigo and I were not moving or connecting. Yet, for me, everything was happening. I was bombarded with internal signals and stimulation, which I was intent to communicate to Amigo.

Being a highly sensitive person, I often found I would unconsciously pick up feelings that others were experiencing and then take them on as if they were mine. Years of being on a conscious path had helped me with this, and sometimes in a group situation, I would be challenged to keep my own "feeling" space. As I worked with Amigo, I let go of having to *understand* what I was feeling and simply focused on *being fully present*, without reacting to the strong sensations and feelings that were running through my body.

Every time I took myself through the process of listening to my body and communicating those findings to Amigo, the sensations in my body subsided a little more. The more I acknowledged what was happening in my body instead of focusing on wanting to change my experience or run away, my body would continue to shift, allowing the fear to dissolve. The way through my fear was to be fully involved with the sensation of it. I reconnected to a deep, primal, instinctive aspect of my being from which I had long ago disconnected. What we resist persists. By removing the resistance in my own experiences, my body began to relax. Running away was not the answer. The fear would have stayed with me, locked in every cell of my body. Being present to my feelings and fears allowed me to move through the sensations, out of fear and into my legs and feet, into my grounding. I grounded my body and opened my heart.

Amigo responded by approaching me, dropping his head to my feet, and moving his lips. He was relaxing into the moment and digesting what was happening. My presence was opposite that of the rough drug runners of his past. Instead of me pushing into his space and forcing him to do what he did not want to do while holding aggressive, passive aggressive, angry, or negative energy as his past handlers had, I was containing my emotions, being honest about them, and standing in my own space.

The fear in my body continued to subside. It was very powerful for me to be in my fear, admit it, and see how Amigo responded. His body was next to mine, his fuzzy coat just a hand's reach away. It was all I could do not to reach out to touch him. I knew better. I knew I needed to respect his space. Instead, I watched his lips soften and move, reflecting the decrease in my internal stress level.

Before coming to this ranch, Amigo's life had been full of abuse and disrespect. In his past, humans had little respect for his boundaries or his horse spirit. He had been used solely for the purpose of human gain. He had coped by shutting down or lashing out, a past I shared with him. I was matched with a horse that reflected my own challenges with boundaries, respect, and trusting others. Amigo taught me how to establish and determine my boundaries.

My desire to make physical connection overrode my logical mind. I slowly reached out to touch Amigo. His head flashed around, and I heard his teeth snap. He kept his head turned and stared at me. I gently and firmly placed my hand on his cheek, his warm coat under my hand. It rested there as we looked at each other. I did not feel completely safe with him, so I softly moved his face farther away, asking him to respect me. In my thoughts I very firmly instructed him that I would work with him and be with him *only* if he respected this boundary. He was not allowed to nip at me at all. I, in return, would not reach out to stroke him. I held my stance with intention deeply seated in every cell of my body. His head dropped slightly, with a nod, as if to say, yes, we have an agreement. I removed my hand and stood still. A wave of compassion flooded my heart, a space I had not felt in a long time, as I reflected on his past. In him I saw reflected a part of myself—angry with others, not able to trust. I told him I was sorry that he had been so mistreated and told him he would always be safe as long as he was on this ranch.

Amigo's head dropped again, and he began to lick his lips and chew. He continued to think about and process around my actions and behavior. Simultaneously, the stress decreased in my body. My legs felt normal, and the fear was gone. I began to walk away from Amigo, just to see how he might respond. He turned and followed me, smelling my footsteps, ready to learn and partner with me. We walked around the round pen. He did not try to nip me again. My fear had diminished. My body felt light, and my legs moved with ease. A wave of happiness swept through my body. A smile came across my face. Within just ten minutes I had released deep fear and made a connection with this horse, a horse that had his own issues with humans. Now we could move forward, slowly, with a mutual understanding. It would be a fine line to walk with Amigo, as his history of abuse was long and deep. He had been shown little care and respect in his drug-running days. To trust again would take some time for both of us.

These lessons have remained with me. Now I see myself setting boundaries and owning my emotional and physical space with others. In fact, two years after this event, in the equine-based learning work I now facilitate with my coaching clients, boundaries, respect, and emotional awareness are common themes of personal and professional development. Because of my empathetic sensitivity, I often unconsciously feel and take on the emotions of others. Amigo helped me to reclaim my own ability to feel and also to own my personal space, even when I might feel fearful. He helped me to stand in my space, even with fear present in my body, and make a powerful request. He also demanded that I do the same for him and that I respect his personal space.

I believe the work I did with Amigo helped me release dark drug secrets that were stored away and old emotions I held around my relationships with money and my self-esteem. These old layers needed to be peeled away in order for me to step into my life's passion and work. Without willingness to look at my mistakes, I could not have freed the energy I was using to hide them in shame. Looking at the darker sides of our past, our present, and our being helps us to heal the wounds, shift the behaviors, and become more whole, to return to the joy we are meant to have.

It is not uncommon for coaching clients to experience similar situations and challenges. When they are on the threshold of the path of their correct livelihood, an old emotional pattern, belief, or experience that is holding them back surfaces. Often, their issues center around heart-related challenges: self-esteem, self-respect, the ability to receive, and being worthy of money and love. Time and time again I witness the mysterious way each client chooses one particular horse from the whole herd to work with . The horse selected always turns out to be the perfect horse and best teacher to aid the client in healing his/her heart, exposing limiting beliefs or learning a life lesson. By becoming present in the presence of a large, sensitive animal, a gateway to consciousness opens and releases the next necessary piece of healing. When in the presence of a horse who teaches, we can no longer hide the dark sides of the subconscious, which influence every decision we make, from the world and, worst of all, from ourselves.

The old wounds of life cannot be denied and packed away in a closet when a person ventures out to do their authentic work in the world. Nor do we need to spend years in therapy to move past the wounds. The simultaneous integration of mind, body, and spirit brings forth greater levels of well-being and aliveness, something that talk-based therapy, and often coaching conversations, fall short of achieving. Yet sharing space with the thousand-pound presence of a horse elicits this integration with grace.

To achieve our passion, mission, or life's calling, we must be willing to look at the dark side of our history and being. These dark secrets, shadow sides, memories, traumas, and thoughts must come to awareness and sift through our minds and how we experience them in our body. Vital life force energy is wasted when dark memories are packed away in the closet of our subconscious. As soon as we release them we can recapture that energy and refocus it on the path we desire. It is the discovery of our darkness that allows more energy to come back into light. The two are side by side on the path of consciousness.

To befriend the dark side, or dark horse, allows us more power to dance with our white side, or white horse. The energy of the white horse illuminates our soul and gives permission for our authentic self and life purpose to emerge in the physical world. We all long for this connection to our dancing, white horse—the return to wholeness, the purity of nature and joy. Are we willing to heal our dark horse energy to get it? To have it? Do you dare?

Four years later, after completing my apprenticeship program, I returned to Linda Kohanov's ranch to facilitate a program for anxious and eager individuals seeking to understand themselves, just as I had years before, through my experience with Amigo. My team of facilitators began to gather up the horses to be used for the day. Naturally I offered to get Amigo. Since the initial healing session I had had with Amigo, I had only handled him once or twice. It had been a full year since I had handled him at all. I had watched him with others and witnessed him coming into his own as a teacher. The Epona-trained handlers continued to give him great respect and allow his boundaries, letting him decide on engagement. He was treated with kindness. This continuous respect had paid off immensely. Amigo had reclaimed the parts of his lost spirit. He was stronger, healthier, and more trusting. If Amigo had been placed in a different situation, with a person who did not understand his need for healing and respect his boundaries, he most likely would have been labeled a bad, difficult, or dangerous horse, and his life quality would have continued to deteriorate.

As I walked out to the pasture, my thoughts swept back to our session years before and how powerful it had been for me on so many different levels. A gentle breeze off the desert floor caressed my back as I walked about twenty feet into the pasture. Amigo stood another fifty feet away. He looked good. He looked content and at home.

I stopped, stood still, took a breath, and felt the sensations in my body. I sensed the fullness of my hips and the vibration of aliveness in my legs. I took a deep breath into my heart, feeling the expansion, warmth, and life. The early morning sun warmed the back of my hair, and the birds were busy with song. Amigo turned and looked at me. In my mind I said, "Come, my friend Amigo, it is time again for you to be the great teacher you are." Amigo walked to me, softly and directly. Arriving at my side, he lowered his head toward the halter I was holding, poking his head into it and almost pulling it out of my hand. A smile spread across my face. I wanted to throw my arms around his cute fuzzy neck. I didn't. I knew to respect him and to respect his personal space. On this occasion we turned and walked together.

How time and love can heal our wounds! There is always potential for every situation to get better, for people to grow and learn a new way of life. It takes one moment of time, and only one moment of time, for a choice to be made and a new direction of life to begin. It takes courage: courage to trust the intentions of others, the courage to be vulnerable. Amigo had done much healing in the past four years, and so had I.

"His is a power enhanced by pride, a courage heightened by challenge.
His is a swiftness intensified by strength, a majesty magnified by grace.
His is a timeless beauty touched with gentleness, a spirit that
calls our hearts to dream."

—Unknown

Fly

Fall in Boulder is my favorite time of the year, and part of me was sad to be leaving town for even a week during the peak foliage color. My daily walks with my dog Suki brought a sense of connection and relaxation into my life. She and I were bonded tightly, and I didn't want to leave her either. I liked my daily routine of working at home, walking in the afternoon, and returning to work for a few more hours.

The excitement about my trip arrived with my first sight of the airport. I was traveling to Calgary, Canada, to present my Mind Body Method coaching process to riders and their horses. A door had opened for me to facilitate riders learning deeper levels of energy and self-awareness with their horses. I felt great gratitude for how my life was beginning to unfold.

As I passed through customs, I walked through another door in my life. A client of mine, Terri, was responsible for this door being opened. Terri and I had been working over the phone for well over six months. In our time together, I had coached Terri on how to manage her emotions and constructively utilize her energy levels to create the life she wanted. Terri, a very experienced horsewoman and skilled dressage rider, was also a riding coach and a Life Coach. In addition she practiced nutritional consulting and offered years of professional corporate experience. Terri answered her coaching phone call one day and announced that the work that we were doing together was transforming not only her life, but also her relationship with her horses. She saw great potential in bringing my Mind Body Method coaching approach directly to her own clients. By that time I had met Hope and had begun to explore the potential for personal and professional development for individuals through engaging with horses.

I was ecstatic about the opportunity to travel to Canada and work with riders. Terri had arranged four days of private sessions and a workshop for us. I asked her, "But what will I do?" to which she replied, "Everything you do with me on our coaching calls." Nine months after our discussion, she greeted me at the airport. By this time I had also had my profound experience with Amigo and had been volunteering with the equine-assisted learning program for several months. In addition I had been leasing a horse to continue to improve my ground and riding skills. I felt more ready than when we first talked. The dream was about to become a reality.

When Terri and I originally met, I had been teaching individuals how to become more integrated in mind, body, and emotions by using the chakra system as a model for growth. During this period of time I had written my first book, *Pathway to a Radiant Self, A Journey of Growth and Discovery with the Chakras.* My intention in writing the book was to provide my coaching clients with a system to access their passion and life vitality from the inside of their being to their outside life, or world. The origin of the chakra system and its philosophies are based in the ancient Hindu religion. My intention was to simplify the concepts in the system so that people could access the teachings.

The chakra system involves seven distinct energy centers that line up vertically along the spinal column, from the base of the spine to the top of the head. These centers do not exist on a physical level, like the heart, stomach, or lungs, but instead on an energetic level. Imagine a small tornado swirling and moving air as it gathers particles. Each energy center could resemble this image—a mass of energy moving with momentum, everything flowing in the same direction. Each energy center has its own specific focus for growth and healing. These topics, or teachings, include being grounded and secure and trusting the flow of one's life, being of service, and personal power and responsibility through love, truth, creativity, intuition, emotional well-being, and spiritual awakening.

Terri and I not only became very intrigued with how each horse pointed to a significant energy center (chakra) on the rider's body, but we also noticed that each client would process a challenge in the area corresponding to the teachings this ancient system maps out. So many things began to tie together and make sense, yet we never expected any of this to transpire as it did. The horses would stand calmly, anticipating our ability to take note of their communication, and then they held the space for the shifts to happen.

The colors in Calgary were as beautiful as Boulder. We drove for about an hour to a very rural area. Rolling hills, narrow roads, and hay pastures filled the landscape. In the distance the Canadian Rockies owned the skyline, graced by an early dusting of snow. Their peaks pierced the horizon, jetting vertically to the sky. We worked two days on Terri's property, enjoying the mild temperatures and blue skies. The last two days, the temperatures dramatically dropped. Instead of enjoying the warmer breezes and blowing leaves, we were bundled in layers and hugging cups of coffee between sessions.

The owner of the barn arranged for the facility to be fully available to us and only us. We would have no distractions from other boarders. She offered a quiet container for us to work with others. Inside the barn was as cold as the outside, if not colder. Unaccustomed to standing in a cold arena, my feet were cold and numb before long. I had not expected and was not prepared for the temperatures to drop so severely in September. But every day brought us another success with Terri's clients, many of the sessions leaving us deep in amazement, stunned and humbled by the horses' willingness to participate and their ability to help.

Terri's depth of knowledge of her clients and their horses and of horse safety in general created a space for amazing things to transpire for many of her clients. My many years of working with people in deep levels of process and breakthrough added a wonderful structure to hold the clients' processes. Together we brought years of diverse experience and thousands of client sessions. During my time in Calgary, Terri and I worked as a team. As I coached each of our clients through the Mind Body Method coaching process, Terri stood close by and kept an eye on the horse and anything else outside my awareness. Ultimately she was my second pair of eyes, and she energetically held a space around us that became grounded and sacred; a space that allowed her clients to drop into a deep process with me, after only having met me just minutes before.

We witnessed several themes with almost every client. The first and perhaps the most astounding thing was how each horse responded to and communicated with the rider. Typically I would begin the session by discussing her goals with the rider and what she thought might be holding her back from achieving them. During this initial discussion the rider would be focused on me. Her horse would lean in and place its nose on a part of the rider's body, holding it there just long enough for Terri and me to notice. The rider would often unconsciously dismiss her horse, pushing the horse's nose away and continuing to focus on our conversation. Terri and I would always note the message and communication the horse had offered. Often the rider was blind to the horse's communication.

Eventually, usually later in the session, as clients became more body-centered in their awareness, their attention would go to the same place on their body their horse had previously placed its nose. As they focused on this area, they would experience energetic and emotional shifts as important insights and information emerged from this area of their body. All of the clients at that time were unaware that their horse had pointed to the very same spot. Ultimately each one of them would release old beliefs or trauma memory or generate the feeling of personal power from the area of the body where their horse had pointed. Every rider became more body-centered, releasing limited energy that was locked in their body and affecting their riding. Every rider brought forth more confidence and honesty in the moment, regaining an element of personal power. The result was a harmony within their body that then transferred to the horse. The horse would soften, drop its head, and begin to lick and chew during these key moments of shifting. After the shift was complete, the rider and horse would move with lightness and connection not previously experienced. The difference was visible and palpable.

A woman named Connie and her horse Fly came for a session. Connie was a massage therapist, short, with wavy reddish brown hair and light freckles sprinkled on her fair complexion. Fly was unassuming, average in appearance, a flea-bitten brown color, her eyes soft and energy relaxed. As we began the check-in, Fly bumped against Connie's shoulder twice. Connie brushed her away both times, mentioning that she wasn't really sure why she brought this horse to work with. Fly was not her favorite, but at the last minute she had decided to load her in the trailer and bring her. Fly snuck her nose around and placed it on the back of Connie's shoulder. Again, Connie brushed her away as she eagerly communicated her goals to me.

I asked Connie to walk around the arena with Fly on the lead line, as I thought it might be good to see how they moved together on the ground before we did any mounted work. Connie moved from a walk to a trot as she remained beside Fly. She headed down the arena, away from us. She appeared stiff between her shoulder blades. It was as if a steel rod ran horizontally between the two sides of her body; there was no flexibility. Connie held a lot of tension in that area. Rounding the end of the arena, she and Fly moved directly toward me, transitioning from a walk to a trot. My focus softened to take in not only the details of each being, but also to allow the energy between them and how they followed together to become apparent. This softer, wide-angle view, similar to how horses see, allowed me to take in information that my logical mind might have rejected or dismissed.

As they moved toward me I could not take my eyes off Connie's right shoulder. Connie then mounted her horse, and they traveled around the arena, circling once, rounding the far end of the arena, then heading down the center straight toward me. Again I softened my gaze, allowing my view to broaden. This time I could not take my eyes off Fly's right shoulder. It appeared as if Fly was almost lame, or at least she favored her left side. Something about the right side was off. I asked Terri if she was seeing the same thing. She too sensed that something was off in Fly's right shoulder. Clearly, Fly was not extending her gait fully. In addition, there was a lack of connection between Connie and Fly. The flow was not there. It felt like there was a lack of trust and honesty; the naturalness that one sees between a horse and rider that are well fitted was missing.

As I began to take Connie through the Mind Body Method focusing process, she soon dropped into her body and began to connect to the areas of her body that seemed most alive with energy. Each time she gave her full focus to the area of her body that naturally drew her attention. She focused in and became fully present to the area—the sensations that were present and the feeling and emotion she associated with it. Finally, she asked for a message to arise from that area of her body. In between each of the body-centered check-in segments, Connie and Fly walked along, with Terri and me close beside her.

During the third body-centered check-in, Connie's attention went to her right shoulder. Significant emotion began to arise. Connie then told me that she and Fly had had an accident. They had stumbled and fallen, and Connie had dislocated her right shoulder. My intuitive hit was confirmed. Connie was holding some type of pain energy, physical or emotional, in her shoulder area. Connie had the shoulder injury and Fly, sensitive to the rider's body energy, like all horses, was reflecting the pain that Connie was holding in her shoulder through her own body, in her own shoulder.

Tears sprang to Connie's eyes. Fly started pawing the ground, shifting her weight side to side, her shifting becoming more intense. I asked Connie to dismount and stand next to her horse, sensing that it would be best for her to stand on her legs and ground her own body, instead of Fly doing that for her. Fly was a sensitive horse. With the level of energy moving through Connie, I did not feel it safe or appropriate for Fly to have to manage that energy.

Once she was standing, I coached Connie through the emotions that were emerging. As we talked through the process, Connie revealed some past hurt around being loved and accepted and ultimately being cared for and supported. At that very significant moment, when Connie was expressing her absolute truth about the situation, Fly leaned forward and softly pressed her nose to Connie's heart. Unconsciously, Connie pushed her away. I asked Connie if she was aware of what she had just done. She was not. She was unconscious that she had literally pushed her equine partner out of her space when she had reached her nose toward her to softly touch her heart. Dumbfounded, she confessed that she pushed everyone in her life away, and that was why she did not feel love and support. Her eyes filled with tears as she confessed that she felt she couldn't trust or let anyone close to her heart.

As Connie explored other ways that she shut people and her horse out of her life, she released the stress and emotions from her heart area. I invited her to stand a moment and to breathe and allow Fly to do as she pleased. Fly leaned in and again placed her nose on Connie's heart. Together they stood as Fly's warm breath brushed against Connie's coat.

The heart area was the same area that Fly had gracefully pointed to at the very start of the session. The heart center is one of the seven chakra centers. This center teaches how to balance self-love and love for others and to trust intimacy. We spoke about what Connie wanted and how she could create that with Fly. She mounted her horse. Centering again as her tears dried, she began to walk her horse. I coached her to breathe deeply into her body and to move her arms and shoulders upwards, then horizontally to her sides, twisting both ways to look behind her. These processes were developed by Sally Swift and can be found in her book *Centered Riding*. The stretches helped Connie access the physical energy that may not have been released in her emotional process. To the far end of the arena she went. Coming back toward me in the center, she moved into a trot. She moved with ease. Fly's shoulders moved equally, neither compensating for the other; the imbalance I had sensed before was gone. Connie continued to work with Fly, each time gaining more suppleness and flow as they began to move together in unison. The stress of her shoulder, her distrust, her blocked and protected heart had been released. She could now begin to trust again. She could reestablish trust in her horse. She could see her patterns with people and begin to move toward creating intimacy versus loneliness. She had shifted from holding stiffness in her body and fear in her heart, toward being a relaxed rider, feeling and connecting with her partner below her.

A year later I returned to Calgary and worked with Connie again. Connie showed up bright and full of life force for her session. She looked like a different person. This time we focused purely on aligning her whole being to manifest and attract a loving partner for her. The bulk of her session was done with her mounted on her horse. While mounted she imagined a time in the future when her perfect partner was present in her life. I coached her to pretend that the scene she was seeing was real, allowing her imagination to spring forth. She sat high on her horse as he held her, patiently waiting. She told me how she saw a man on horseback and that they were riding together. The fields were green and the trees in bloom. The sun was shining, and they were laughing and cantering across the open field.

As she held this image in her mind and felt the experience in her whole being, I asked her to open her eyes and ask her horse to walk. The lateral movement of her horse's back stimulated her spinal column, nervous system, and brain. With every step her body was becoming limber and loose, allowing the integration. The more clearly she held the image and feeling state of what she desired, the more the subconscious body experienced it. As she moved through the walk to a trot, she continued to integrate and hold the warm feeling of being loved in her body. She felt her heart expanding and opening to the world around her. All false beliefs and resistance to the possibilities fell away. She literally reprogrammed and realigned her whole being to what she wanted in her life. One year later she was dating a fabulous man and having the time of her life. He, too, loved horses, and they were enjoying riding together.

"Horses change lives. They give our young people confidence and self-esteem. They provide peace and tranquility to troubled souls—they give us hope!"
—Toni Robinson

Stone

Another client's story from that four-day period in Calgary continues to touch my heart every time I think of her. A young female rider named Sarah, with her horse, Stone, through her willingness to work with me, was able to release limiting perceptions and thoughts she was holding about her ability to achieve her dreams in the world. Her story demonstrates that regardless of age, the foundational piece that will profoundly affect our ability to reach our potential lies within the mind and is held in the subconscious of the body. When we conquer limiting self-talk and instead engage the voice of possibility and confidence, our courage and authenticity come pouring forth.

Stone was a magnificent horse. Solid black and 16.2 hands high, his well-bred Thoroughbred body reflected his majestic qualities. He came from the highest quality of bloodlines. His soft, strong demeanor indicated service and dependability. A horse with a gentle nature, there was little that could shake his solid core. The name Stone suited him just fine.

Sarah was a beautiful young lady, her long, straight, ash-colored hair framing her young, innocent face. Sarah was just sixteen and the proud owner of this horse. Her dream was to compete in the Olympics, flying on the wings of her horse through every technical course. She and Stone loved to jump.

In her budding womanhood, Sarah was challenged by stresses at home. Her family owned the horse farm where Terri and I facilitated sessions. It was a busy place, with lots of people and horses coming and going. Although Sarah had the privilege of riding whenever she wanted, that luxury did not come without cost. A stressed-out mother and a rebellious sister affected Sarah's own self-esteem and ability to reach the heights of performance she desired.

Sarah suffered from guilt and self-inflicted shame. Guilt, the demon of our potential and passions, pulls us into sabotaging behaviors and creates doubts about our abilities and rights to own our power and greatness. Shame, the emotion that accompanies guilt, convinces us that what we are doing, and sometimes even who we are, is wrong. Guilt comes when we conclude that something we did was wrong or bad. Shame is the feeling we carry in our body and hearts when we believe that *we* are bad.

Sarah and Stone entered the arena for our first session. Their invisible yet obvious bond was pregnant with potential. They were surrounded by an aura of anticipation. Like the moment before a first kiss, it felt like something was about to emerge and shift in their partnership. Stone remained solid, unchanged by my presence. In fact, his demeanor supported my own ability to stay grounded and focused on the session. I could feel Sarah's slight edge of nervousness. She knew very little about me or what might happen in our time together. I too knew little of her, but I knew that what needed to transpire would be perfect. Stone, firm, solid, and secure, a quiet spirit, stood next to her; his body brushed softly against hers.

Sarah told of her desire to be the best rider she could be and to someday be an Olympic contender. Yet she found herself unable to get beyond a certain height in her jumping. She would stall or completely avoid the challenging jumps. She was not feeling the depth of her connection with Stone, as she wanted. She yearned to feel the "oneness," the loss of boundaries, the merging of two beings moving toward the same goal. She wanted to experience harmony and flow and be able to move through their hurdles and challenges with ease. She wanted to trust the process.

As Sarah shared her vision, Stone softly dropped his head. He slowly curved his neck and softly placed his nose onto Sarah's solar plexus. The solar plexus is the energy center of personal power and will, governed by one's mental activities, or how a person thinks and speaks to herself. This slight but very important gesture sparked my curiosity to find out what Stone was pointing to by placing his nose on her belly. What was Sarah holding there that was ready to move and be released and would allow her the connection she longed for?

My intuition told me to have Sarah mount Stone and ride around the ring. Stone's power and fluidity were like swells in the ocean, consistent, soothing, yet coming from a vast depth. I sensed that Stone was holding back a bit, and Sarah seemed to hold more energy in her head than her body. There was a clear energetic disconnection between Sarah's upper and lower body. Sarah was a fine rider, experienced and skilled, yet even from a distance I sensed the subtle disconnect between her and Stone. I asked her to move closer, and when she and Stone walked in smaller circles around me I asked her key questions to help her center in her body and increase her awareness of her energy flow. "Sarah, as you move with Stone, bring your awareness to your chest. What do you feel there?" "What are you feeling in your hips?" "What do you sense in your legs and your feet?" "What part of your body are you noticing the most?" Each time Sarah moved her awareness into her body and listened to the sensations she was experiencing, she became more relaxed and present in the moment, and she settled down into her saddle and into the session. They stopped next to me.

Sarah began to talk about her family and her trepidation about outshining her sister, Lori. Sarah did not feel she had the right to be the brilliant young woman that she was when her dearest female companion was spiraling downward into behaviors that caused disharmony in the family. Her sister's grades were dropping, and she was getting into trouble after school. Sarah worried that if she shined, then what would happen to Lori? Would she become more rebellious? Would she grow to hate Sarah and her success? On top of that, pressures from her mother, her school, and her duties at the barn were stressing Sarah. The tone of Sarah's voice was constricted, her energy was tight, and one negative statement after another continued to pour out of her mouth.

I reflected back to Sarah the very statements I was hearing. Sarah did not realize how much negativity she had been holding inside her mind and how it was affecting her posture. My guess was she seldom talked to anyone about her feelings toward her sister's situation.

Our discussion led us to explore three very important voices within every person: the inner voice, the outer voice, and the critical voice. The inner voice we hear from deep within our being, from the heart. The critical voice comes from inside our head and is negative or judging. The outer voice is what we choose to speak with others. Yet each voice is different. Sarah and I talked about the importance of listening to her inner voice, the one that no one else hears, but that often speaks loudly and clearly. This voice is soft and supportive, sometimes direct and to the point, but always there to support us and protect us and ultimately lead us on our journey. It comes from the authentic part of our being that wishes to guide us on our right path.

The voice of the critic has nothing good to say. It is the voice that puts one down; makes us feel "less than"; compares us to others; and punishes and reprimands us, always unjustly. This voice makes people feel *bad* about who they are or what they are doing. The voice of the critic keeps us feeling guilty or shameful. It keeps us small and distant from our own greatness or power. This voice plants negative limiting beliefs into our subconscious. It is based in fear and pulls us away from our authentic state of being.

We also explored the importance of Sarah's outer voice—the language and tone she uses to talk about herself and the world around her. I stressed how her words influence and ultimately create how she feels and how she participates in present and future situations. With every verbal articulation, she creates her experience in the world. The outer voice reflects how we feel internally and which internal voice runs our life.

Sarah and I talked about each of these voices and how they were showing up in her life. Sarah realized that her critical voice kept her feeling bad about herself. It was keeping her small to protect her sister. Because she was good, Sarah felt bad. She was a good student, a good daughter, and a good rider. Her erroneous thinking was, "If I wasn't so good, my sister wouldn't have to feel so bad."

Stone stood patiently; soon his head dropped and relaxed. He brushed his massive body against mine, as if to offer me support and grounding. His licking and chewing revealed he was keyed in on the authenticity of our conversation. Sarah was getting real with herself and into the guts of her issue, as painful as it might have been. Stone continued to be the rock that was energetically holding us all together.

I encouraged Sarah to create a sentence to support her and Stone in creating success, to replace her negative thought patterns and the voice of the critic. After a few seconds, she said her affirming sentence out loud: "I am me, and that is great." "Wonderful," I replied. Next I instructed Sarah to say her words out loud as she and Stone moved around the circle in a walk. Softly Sarah spoke her chosen words. They were barely audible. "Louder, Sarah, I want to hear you." Her voice became louder as she and Stone circled around me in a nice walk. Sarah focused on matching the words of her voice to the movement of Stone's body. Each footstep created a steady rhythmic beat. Stone continued to walk, steady, solid, and reliable. "Louder!" I demanded. "Sarah, say it like you mean it." Each time Sarah's voice grew stronger. Each time she continued her mantra: "I am me, and that is great."

Her body softened in her saddle and began to meld with Stone's movement, enhancing the side-to-side movement the horse provided. With each side-to-side movement, her hips rotated. This movement created in riding a horse stimulates the rider's spinal column and the fluid that flows up and down from the base of the spine to where it connects to the base of the head. This fluid nourishes the whole body. In addition, this stimulation to the spinal column also stimulates all of the nerves connected to it, reaching out to all of the limbs. This in itself can be highly healing and stimulating for individuals with any physical handicaps. This motion also profoundly affects the connection between mind and body, stimulating new thought processes and connecting them to the deeper part of the body and the subconscious aspect of one's being.

I coached Sarah further, raising my voice each time to encourage her to raise her own. "Sarah, use your body. Breathe into it, *own it!*" In her next breath Sarah sang her mantra loud and strong. "I am Me, and that is Great!" Finally, her words rang true. The deep resonance and strength of her conviction filtered out any remaining doubts in her mind or in mine.

In that moment a wave of energy moved rapidly through my body. My empathic abilities gave me a clear sign of what she experienced. Starting at my solar plexus, heat flushed through me, simulating in me the power of her work. Sarah was sitting high and straight in the saddle, tears of relief pouring down her face. She had dared to claim, or reclaim, part of herself. She acknowledged her power and owned her greatness—a moment that many of us long for, yet never achieve.

I asked her where she felt her greatness and her power. Her hand moved to her stomach, the very spot that Stone had pointed out at the beginning of the session. She expressed the heat and expansion she felt there. She had activated her center of power, and with every syllable more truth poured forth, through her voice and her body, with Stone's support and help. Terri and I offered cheers of support as Sarah continued around the circle, the power of her truth pouring forth in every syllable of her declaration.

Sarah had made a transformation. Lightness surrounded all of us. Joy and confidence were palpable in the air. Sarah and I continued to work together to help her acknowledge the energy she had released: to recognize the feeling state in her body and to stay with the feeling of her personal power. Sarah reported a greater lightness in her whole body. No longer held back by limitations and doubt, her solar plexus felt stimulated with excitement and possibility. She had fully engaged with the seat of her personal power, located in her solar plexus, influencing her ability to move forward with confidence into the world.

Sarah appeared to have grown taller, her energy brilliant and radiant. With ease, she and Stone began to make big loops around the arena. Together they flowed in unison: Stone with greater lightness in his step and Sarah with a deep, confident smile of success.

How often do we become small so that someone else is not hurt? How often do we let the doubts of others and the stresses of everyday life take us away from our greatness? When does our critical voice take over, limiting our ability to achieve and shine in the world? It is our right to claim our power, to claim our greatness, and to shine in the brightest way possible.

Marianne Williamson said it best in her book *A Return to Love: Reflections on the Principles of "A Course in Miracles:"*

> *Our deepest fear is not that we are inadequate. Our deepest fear is that we are powerful beyond measure. It is our light, not our darkness, that most frightens us. We ask ourselves, who am I to be brilliant, gorgeous, talented and fabulous? Actually, who are you not to be? You are a child of God. Your playing small doesn't serve the world. There's nothing enlightened about shrinking so that other people won't feel insecure around you. We were born to manifest the glory of God that is within us. It's not just in some of us; it's in everyone. And as we let our own light shine, we unconsciously give other people permission to do the same. As we are liberated from our own fears, our presence automatically liberates others.*

We always have a choice as to which voice we will listen to. We can side with the voice of the critic or the saboteur and fall into a disempowered state of being. Or we can choose to activate the voice of confidence, honoring our spirit and our right to have joy and reach our goals. Do we dare enter deep into the gut, into the belly of our emotions and energy to create an alignment that moves us to new heights of awareness and realization? Do we dare to own our own magnificence? Do we dare to believe in our God-given potential?

At the end of our session, with new tools to work with, Sarah had shifted her thoughts, her voice, and perspective from limitations into possibilities. She had shifted, from the inside of her body, to the outside world, her belief about herself. She was empowered, and her authentic nature filled the entire arena space. She had come back to herself. She was beaming from ear to ear as she and her magnificent partner, Stone, exited the arena.

My hope is that for the rest of her life Sarah will remember the power of the moment she claimed her life and connected to her authentic self. I see her recalling it every time she hits a limitation, remembering how to engage with the inner voice and to speak of her potential and truth, to speak in the manner that honors her self. For the rest of her life she will always have this visceral experience with her partner Stone as a cornerstone of self-love and empowerment. Ultimately, I hope that someday she and Stone reach greater heights in their jumping and that they are smiling as they receive the gold at the Olympics.

"Through the days of love and celebration and joy, and through the dark days of mourning—the faithful horse has been with us always."

—Elizabeth Cotton

Flash

More and more opportunities for working with horses and humans continued to emerge for me. Without my own horse or herd, my work took me to various locations and exposed me to many people and types of horses.

The power of the horse to connect to people and reflect, heal, empower, and communicate through body language and self-expression is crystal clear to me. I have been astounded at the level at which they are willing to give, and continue to give, over and over, even while living in less than desirable conditions. Is it the nature of the horse to give so much, to be of great service?

In the winter of 2004, my journey took me to a remote part of Arizona, an area called Skull Valley, just outside of Prescott. I rented and shared a small house for the winter with a friend, her horses, the owner's horses, three dogs, and a cat. Unfortunately it was the wettest winter in a long time. The six-mile dirt road to the house was a mud slick for weeks. The dry wash beside the property turned into a raging river, rising over five feet. Its force ate away at the steep banks, taking yards of pasture and fencing downstream. At night I would venture out in the pouring rain to check on it, wondering just how high it could rise, in awe of the dramatic forces of the desert. Day after day the horses stood in muddy stalls. Creating small ditches to drain the water was useless. Finally the weather broke, before the horses had to be moved to higher ground. The desert became a desert again, and the daylight of spring stretched into the early evenings.

For a workshop I had planned, I had chosen a spot to build a round pen in the large, rocky, and sandy pasture sheltered by the few surrounding cottonwoods. Views of the mountains to the west created expansion; the now-dry riverbed was to the south and the gate to the round pen to the east. It felt private but was still close enough to be convenient to the stalls and the meeting area. My landlord had offered to help with the project and had cleared the area of rocks and debris.

A warm breeze promised spring as I stood in the center of the round pen a few days before the workshop, feeling energy and excitement for the workshop build within me. Still, sometimes deep inside, I longed for the knowledge that I was on the right path. I wanted to be sure that I would not regret turning down the high-paying corporate opportunity offered just days before. It seemed I always chose the occupations that challenged the status quo in society. First it was massage therapy, then polarity therapy, onwards to Life Coaching, and now using horses as teachers with my coaching work. I felt like I was living on the edge of reality.

My eyes searched the sky for a sign, some sign, any sign, that the universe could offer me, that the choices made were the right choices, that there was an unknown yet powerful reason for me to be doing this work in the world. "Give me a sign," I asked, "give me a clear sign." My eyes dropped to the ground on my left. There, resting in the sand, was a black obsidian arrowhead. The rains had moved the sand, and sitting perfectly balanced on the grains of colorful sand was the arrowhead. How many times had I, or my landlord, walked past it in the last week as we were preparing the round pen? How could we have missed it?

The sharp edges pressed into my palm as I picked it up and held it. A smile spread across my face. I was reminded that there is something much more powerful and majestic than the physical human form that guides us on our path. Some may call this force of energy "spirit," "the universe," "angels," "the divine," or "God." This mysterious matrix evoked within me a deep sense of connection with the world beyond me. The little black arrow confirmed in my head what I had known in my heart. I was to trust my decision and follow the flow of my life's work.

The unpredictability of spring did not let up for the workshop. Snow spat, and temperatures dropped. It did not matter to the participants; they were excited to explore and experience the horses. Each time we ventured outside, the clouds parted and the sun shone.

We had five horses to work with: four Arabians and one Quarter Horse. Arabians are known for being great teachers in this line of work because of their keen awareness, intelligence, and sensitivity. Our sessions started with Flash, a twenty-two-year-old Arabian mare who did not enjoy being in the confined area of the round pen.

Before the workshop, I brought her to the round pen to work to see how she would respond. Flash was an overweight, docile, and slow-moving mare. In the round pen she became stressed out, pacing and circling the pen. It was difficult to help Flash bring her energy down into a walk, and getting a halt was impossible. Sensing her stress, I left the gate open and through my mind communicated to her that she could leave if that's what she wanted to do. Flash stopped in her tracks. I approached and stroked her neck for comfort. After a few seconds, she walked out of the round pen and then stood outside; she glanced back at me. In that moment I promised Flash that if a participant selected her to work with that she would always be able to leave the round pen; the gate would be open. After a long pause, Flash's eye lingering on mine, she turned her head and walked back to her stall and food.

An "open gate" policy is not the usual way to facilitate equine-based learning sessions. Most of the work I had done up to this point was in larger arenas. These arenas gave more options for the horse to move or to create distance. The round pen offered a more intimate setting for a group workshop. Obviously, it was too confined and intimate for Flash. Her history was unknown to me; it seemed with her responses that she had had unpleasant experiences in the round pen, an area usually used for training and exercising horses. An exception was made for Flash, and I let the workshop participants know about my agreement with her.

The first woman who chose to work with Flash, Chris, was grieving the loss of her dog. Flash was placed in the round pen with the gate open. She stood patiently. Chris and I stood outside the round pen, and she began to move through the steps of the Mind Body Method process. Immediately Chris's tears began to flow. Flash moved across from the far west side of the round pen to the east side where Chris and I stood. Flash moved her body flush against the fence line just a few feet away from Chris. She stood there silently. Throughout the coaching process, Chris became fully body-centered, even as tears flowed gracefully down her face. She then articulated her intention: "I would like Flash to help me let go of my grief." Flash watched her, unmoving. Chris walked into the round pen.

As Chris moved to the center of the round pen, Flash moved from the edge and stood right next to Chris and exhaled a deep sigh. It was as if Flash was offering her shoulder for Chris to lean on and release her tears. Silently and quietly the two stood together, Chris leaning into Flash and accepting her shoulder. This was not a cathartic release, but instead a graceful letting go. In less than a minute Chris had no more tears to be shed.

I continued to communicate with Chris, offering suggestions and asking key questions to support her process. Flash continued to offer her support without any instruction or direction. It was powerful to witness the depth that Chris went to in her process. It was equally powerful to witness the willingness, softness, and grace that Flash demonstrated in supporting her.

Then the session came to completion. The gate had been open to the round pen the whole time. Flash had no halter or lead line; she was completely free to do as she pleased. As Chris walked out of the round pen, Flash was right by her side. They continued walking side by side to where the rest of the group was waiting to debrief the session. Together they waited, Flash standing patiently, until everyone in the group shared her experience. Chris shared with the group that her time with Flash allowed a very deep level of grief to bubble up from within her. The grief she released was more than the loss of her dog, and it felt very old.

During this whole time, Flash was at liberty and could have run right back to her stall to eat (which she loves to do) at any time. Instead, she chose to stay with Chris until the whole process was complete, giving her full self and attention to Chris. Flash had "joined up" with Chris.

Later that weekend, another participant, Fran, chose to work with Flash. Fran and I also began the coaching process outside of the round pen. Fran had a harder time becoming completely centered and present in the moment. She spoke in metaphors, staying completely in her head, where she obviously felt safe. She wanted to rush through the mind-body centering process—she wanted to get into the round pen and experience Flash.

After a few more minutes of helping Fran center, it was time for her to move into the round pen. As soon as Fran stepped into the round pen, Flash headed toward the gate, peeled out of the round pen, and went straight back to her stall. It was clear to all of us that Flash did not want to be in the round pen or work with this person. Flash could have left at any time while Fran and I were standing on the outer edge. Instead, she waited until the moment Fran stepped into the round pen space.

What made these two sessions so unalike? Why did Flash act so differently with these two people? In my experience, most sessions are unique; as with the two above, each has its own chemistry. Sessions can also be very similar. Sometimes it appears that a particular horse resonates with certain human issues, challenges, or past emotional traumas more than others. The horses that have experienced physical trauma or emotional stress can be good at supporting humans with the same issues. It is as if there is also an emotional resonance, an unspoken understanding or connection. In this case it seemed that Flash resonated with, or was drawn to, people with grief and sadness.

Different horses offer different learning experiences. Some are great at play, pushing boundaries, mirroring another's thoughts or feelings, or holding a space for people to come to the present moment. As I have developed my own herd, I see that each equine member works with people in their own special way. From a wide selection of horses with different life histories and personalities, clients pick the horse that resonates with the learning that is most appropriate for them at that junction of their lives.

One month before the workshop, Flash had worked with me on a grieving issue. I was also grieving the loss of my beloved dog

Suki. Sensing that her departure from the world was coming, I had ignored subtle signs. Thoughts of losing her had begun to enter my mind. I brushed these off as paranoia and fear. She had also started to slow down. I justified this because she was getting older and was now nine—maybe she was becoming mellow in her later years. One morning, as she did her usual stretch in front of me, I sensed grayness in the energy around her, not her usual bright self. I dismissed this thinking as imagination. Two days later Suki was sullen and despondent. Still ready to chase a ball or two, after only one or two tosses she kept her ball and lay down beside me. Again, I brushed it off. I assured myself she had been bitten by a wasp or a random desert insect.

The next day Suki woke with lots of energy, and when she ventured outside she was chasing rodents with her usually vigor. But only two hours later she was limp, a pile of motionless fur, her big sad eyes staring at me. I realized I had ignored the truth I already had sensed. I rushed her to the local vet; the fifty-minute drive felt like an eternity. Suki's image filled my rearview mirror when she sat up to watch her surroundings with glazed-over eyes, and she then lay back on the floor. She was going into shock; my heart raced, and I was scared.

The vet he confirmed what I did not want to hear. Suki had cancerous tumors on her spleen. He could operate, but even if he did, she might have only a few months to live. Panic took over as I fought with my logical mind my fear of facing this reality. In the instant the vet waited for me to decide, my fear surfaced and overcame my heart-based reasoning, I made a decision I have regretted ever since: I asked him to operate.

The vet let me place the mask over her muzzle as she weakly attempted to move away. Soon the anesthesia took hold, and she went limp. I stroked her soft coat and then left her in the hands of the vet, while I sat numb and blank in the waiting room. Suki died on the operating table, came back, and then died again. I knew the moment she had gone to the other side. And in that moment, I knew that I needed to honor her life and what she had brought to me. Her death reminded me of how short life is and confirmed that the high-paying corporate job that had just the week before been offered to me was not my path. Instead I would continue to live a life of risks and bring the work with humans and horses to the world.

The loss of an animal that touches our life with unconditional loyalty and love strikes the core of the heart. Suki had been my companion every day from the moment she came into my life to the moment she left. She taught me more about being present and joyful in the moment than any human companion had. Her spirit, big and alive, willing and daring, loving and forgiving, had filled a void in my life. Animals have an incredible way of capturing one's heart. Their astute observations, of which often we are unaware, teach them to anticipate and know our every move and every thought.

Animals of all types offer unconditional service to humans. Their ability to be completely present with us gives us an experience that we often cannot find in our human relationships. Their unconditional love expands hearts and widens smiles. When they depart this physical life and move into the spirit realm, the void that is left can bring us deep into a grieving process. In that process, they continue to teach, touch, and reconnect us to the experiences that we are offered as spiritual beings having a physical experience. The void was painful for me. Not only had I lost her, but also I regretted not giving her a dignified death. I wished that instead of proceeding with the surgery, I had carried my canine girl down to the river and allowed her a peaceful death in nature, with the sound of water rippling in her ears and the feel of the ground beneath her skin. I continued to grapple with regret, guilt, and the pain of losing her.

Back at home, I went out to the horses' pasture, not really sure what I was seeking but wanting the comfort of being with the horses. I also did not want to use the horses; I did not want to go out and throw myself onto one of them and relieve myself by dumping my emotions onto one of them. This seemed unfair, like a child who becomes the emotional support for an emotionally unbalanced adult. Trapped and powerless, the child does what it needs to in order to deal with the circumstances. The child supports, tolerates, tries to make things better, and eventually closes her heart for protection because her heart lacks the maturity to carry such a burden. I wonder if horses, like a child in a family wanting to please, give beyond what they are capable of or should need to. What impulse is behind their willingness to give?

I walked to the edge of the pasture, let myself through the gate, and stood just inside the fence. The horses on the far side glanced up. In my mind I asked the horses if anyone was willing to say hello. I stood and waited. Flash stood in the distance, her head up, ears forward, facing me. She walked away from the herd toward me. She stopped about four feet away. My eyes began to water. She then walked a circle around me and stopped next to me, her left shoulder next to me. Quietly we stood together. She brought her face next to my closed eyes. I could feel her breath and the flutter of her eyelashes against my check. The tears began to flow. Then she took a step forward, and her shoulder was next to me. I stood still, tears coursing down my cheeks, but fully present. I was shocked that she was there and somewhat lost about how to receive her presence. Flash put all of her weight on her front leg, the leg next to me. She leaned her body against mine; my head came down and rested on her neck, my chest on her shoulder. There we stood for minutes, unmoving except for the comforting soft sway of our bodies. Her heat blended with mine, her firm flesh pressed against mine, and for an instant we were as one, joined in the process. Tears flowed and grief rose in my body like a wave curling and folding back onto itself. My heart expanded as if to stretch the actual size of my chest. Appreciation for Flash mingled with feelings of loss. Suddenly the tears stopped. I was empty. Flash then moved away and crossed the pasture to reconnect to her herd, my silent "thank you" trailing behind her.

I walked back toward the house feeling cleansed—lighter, more present, and in the moment. And the moment no longer saddened me, no longer pulled me into the abyss of grief; rather, the moment was simply that: the moment.

What calls a horse to walk across a pasture and lean against a human, brushing eyelashes and swaying in the winter sun? Why will she stand for two people who shed tears for lost companions and yet flee from another who is challenged in being present? Flash moved toward individuals in the emotional state of grieving, yet she would not acknowledge or work with another individual who was less centered in her body and aware of her emotions and who was not working on an issue related to grief. The fact that Flash also offered her support to me, without any direction, when I was processing my grief was not simply a coincidence. Flash was at full liberty all three times. The pasture area was well over seven acres. She could have moved far away from me, choosing not to be of service, not to connect, and to go back to grazing. [2]

My experience with Flash was not filled with the positive emotions of love and acceptance but the release of a deep loss. However, my

---

2 Dr. Ellen Kaye Gehrke has begun to facilitate a series of scientific studies to gather data on the effects of equine learning sessions with tools and processes created by the Heart Math Institute of California. Gehrke measures the Heart Rate Variability (HRV), the beat-to-beat changes in heart rate during equine sessions, of both the human and the horse. The HRV flow is sensitive to and affected by one's emotional states. In an article written by Kip Mistral for Horse Connection (August 2007), Gehrke experimented with her horses by sitting in a chair with a horse at liberty in her arena. As she sat in the chair, she practiced the Heart Lock-In®, a process developed by the Heart Math Institute that helps an individual sustain focus on positive emotions such as gratitude or love. While she did this, her horses immediately walked over and engaged with her. Several of the horses placed their heads in her lap for the entire period. Through a series of pilot studies Gehrke is finding that the emotional state of the human affects the state of the horse. By using instruments developed by Heart Math, Gehrke was able to see favorable results indicating that horses tend to perceive the HRV in humans and that they reflect that HRV in their own behavior.

Horses naturally live primarily in a coherent state of being, and humans tend to live in incoherent states. A coherent state implies a higher order of the human system, wherein the heart's rhythmic beat plays a superior role in the whole system. The heart's beat influences how the brain processes. The brain in turn controls the cognitive functions, emotions, and autonomic nervous system. When the rate of the heart changes, there are major changes throughout the whole being. Conversely, an incoherent state would be a state of being when all parts of the system are not functioning with a higher level of order and connection. The heart provides higher levels of coherence. Thus, the effects of the state of a human being in relationship to the horse can be profound.

experience was based within my heart, and I was congruent and truthful about my emotional state. I was not hiding or trying to diminish my experience. She was willing to approach my honest state of pain and hurting heart and to hold a space next to me, as if our hearts synchronized together.

Over and over I have seen an invisible attraction that pulls a human and a horse together for this work. It is the universal Law of Attraction in action. This law states that like energy, or similar vibrations, come together. Thus, a wounded and hurt human will be drawn to the horse that shares a similar type of trauma or emotional pain. The human who is playful and exuberant (even if this aspect of themselves has yet to be set free in their person) will be attracted to the horse that displays the same behaviors and characteristics. The person with poor boundaries will work with the horse that pushes boundaries. The horses teach us about our conscious and unconscious emotions and behaviors.

There are programs that employ horses for therapeutic process, learning experiences, and leadership development that do not consider this key element of allowing the horse to be a horse, to give the horse free choice for engagement or detachment. These programs involve horses and humans in the process of doing activities for the sake of learning or exposing the human's blind side. Many of these programs are of great integrity, preparing the clients with the right tools and knowledge, while at the same time being sensitive to the horses' needs and responses. Other organizations put the client in a situation where they are blind to what they are doing. The client is set up with things to do: cleaning hooves, fetching and haltering horses, with little to no instruction. In these instances, the horses look ridiculous; they get frustrated or exhausted. The participants are often humiliated or shamed in the process, and the facilitators use the horse as a tool, solely a means to an end. These programs disregard and disrespect the horse, an animal with a heart five times the size of a human's, who, as a noble creature who offers unique qualities, deserves deep understanding and willing participation in a partnership beneficial to both parties.

I am thankful for a friend who once asked me the question, "Why confine the noble beasts and force them to our will?" I long for a better answer than I can offer. I long to say, "We have not confined them; they are free, they are forever the image of power and freedom."

The reality is that the domesticated horse is confined. The greater question to ask is, "How can we honor the nobility of the horse by maintaining their heroic and spiritual nature when in relationship with humans and in their confinement?" This is a core value, the premise of what I teach. The horse is not here for us to control, manipulate, or dominate. Rather, the horse is here to teach us about power, authenticity, and how to connect and experience the world as separate beings. With completely different approaches to life, we can come together, communicate, and partner at levels unlike any other interspecies relationship. True partnerships of any kind are formed from these qualities. Providing the horse the greatest level of freedom within the confinement of their domestication allows for this.

Kathy's first few riding lessons were bareback on an Appaloosa. Fortunately, she began to wear a helmet before she rode the Trakehner that threw her.

Kathy and her canine companion, Suki, spent many enjoyable days hiking in the Marion Bells area of the Colorado Rockies. Suki's ashes are scattered in the green valley below the mountain pass.

Amigo expresses pent-up energy. Emotion is energy to a horse and, once expressed, a horse returns to grazing. Amigo learned to trust humans after many years of being treated with compassion and respect. *Photo by Maureen Luikart*

Amigo is relaxed and content after a good roll in shavings. An Equine Facilitated Learning Program can also be healing for a horse. *Photo by Kathy Pike*

Hope patiently poses as Kathy snaps a self-portrait. Hope, the first horse Kathy worked with after her accident, befriended Kathy and helped her see how horses can teach humans.

Kathy discovered the power of her Mind Body Method coaching process while working with riders. An advanced level event rider receives coaching to focus her attention inside herself and find her center. Her horse pays attention to her, and a deeper connection is achieved between horse and rider. *Photo by Re Baker*

After several months, Moon begins to settle into his new home in Colorado and his health returns. Moon gains a sense of his new job as a teacher for humans and continues to bond with Kathy. He and Kathy fool around in the pastures on a warm fall day. *Photo by Roberta McGowan*

Individuals travel from all over the world to experience this unique way of connecting with horses. Friendship and communities are formed with like-minded individuals. Left to right back row: Moon, Kathy, Leeanne Kalbaugh, Constance Haldaman, Sandra Sell-Lee, Mari Rubens. Front row: Alejandra Lara and Nancy Peregrine. *Photo by Nancy Peregrine*

Connie and Fly continue to build a trusting relationship. They enjoy a peaceful break among summer flowers in the woods just outside of Calgary.

Susan Gibbs relaxes and connects with her horse Cajun at sunrise on her homestead in Colorado. Cajun is an exceptional teacher for humans. *Photo by Nancy Wilhelms*

Rebec Loring faces her fear of riding horses as Kathy coaches her to stay centered in her body and create focus. Rebec experiences her first ride ever as Moon's reliable presence and strength supports her process. *Photo by Cyle Davenport*

Horses embrace us physically and emotionally. Sensitive and generous, they wrap their being around our hearts and give us a sense of connection. A white horse generously supports Alejandra Lara during a program in Colorado. *Photo by Nancy Peregrine*

Reggie provided Connie with a powerful experience during their equine learning session. He and Connie continue to spend time together in Boulder, Colorado. *Photo by Michael Harvey*

Kathy's learning programs provide the opportunity for people to grow and step into their personal power and authentic expression. Alejandra Lara (left) and Kathy (right) smile with joy during an Equine Facilitated Learning Program. *Photo by Nancy Peregrine*

The Rebel stands proud shortly after being removed from the public lands. His red tag with the number 5298 marked his identity until adopted by Kathy. Named Corazon de la Montana, his heart is as big as a mountain. *Photo by Ginger Kathrens*

Corazon looks back at Kathy as she approaches him in the field. Kathy slows down and becomes present before engaging with him. He walks to her and offers his partnership. Each day their bond grows deeper as Corazon learns more about human ways. *Photo by Nancy Peregrine*

This does not happen in the *doing* to a horse, it happens through *being* and truly understanding the nature of a horse. It is the being, the essence of their spiritual nature, that is the noble state of the horse. When the human is ready to learn, the horse is ready to teach the art of being, regardless if it is an emotional process, a union with nature, or a deeper awareness of self.

"We have almost forgotten how strange a thing it is that so huge and powerful and intelligent an animal as a horse should allow another, far more feeble animal, to ride upon its back."

—Peter Gray

Pearl

Horses don't cry. At least that is what I was told. I disagree. When horses began to come back into my life, I experienced several situations where I observed horses' tears. At that time I had no opinion about the concept of horses crying. Since then, I have witnessed tears fall freely from several different horses' eyes, exposing and releasing a deeper part of their being. A horse may not cry often, but when one does, it is a sacred moment in time.

The first time a horse shared the shedding of a tear in my presence I was very surprised and deeply humbled. I was not actively seeking this experience—why would I? It occurred when I least expected it.

It was one of the last pleasant autumn weekends in Colorado. The aspen trees were still half masked with burnt orange leaves. It would not be long before the trees would be bare and the first snow would fall, blanketing the land. The autumn sun was warm and soft. My deeper instincts, aware of the coming change of season, amplified my desire to soak up every moment of warmth and to breathe deeply the scent of crisp leaves and dried grass before the whiteness arrived.

I had driven from Boulder to Steamboat Springs to visit my friends. One was John, new to the farrier trade, who was accustomed to driving longer distances to reach the customers other farriers did not want to work with. In addition, my long-time friend Becky joined us. The three of us loaded up the SUV and drove some distance on a dirt road that snaked through the foothills. Eventually we reached a clearing. Sun-dried grasses gently bent in the subtle breeze. A dark bay gelding and a white Arabian mare grazed in harmony in the field. The owner of the ranch came out to meet us; she was a pleasant woman, and I sensed ease in her spirit. She introduced us to her horses. The Arabian mare was named Pearl and the second horse was Bailey, to create a duo, "Pearl Bailey." My friend was there to shoe Bailey. We chatted, enjoying the day, as the husband brought Bailey in from the pasture to the round pen.

Everyone watched John begin to shoe Bailey. I felt drawn to Pearl, who was still in the pasture. Pearl's owner told me that they had rescued Pearl from an abusive environment. She was not sure what had happened to Pearl, but she was pretty sure that Pearl had been hit, especially around her neck and head, as she seldom liked anyone to touch her there. It also took Pearl time to warm up to new people.

Pearl was in an area with low string fencing. I walked over and stood at the edge of this fencing, looking at her. She lifted her head and looked at me. I silently invited Pearl to come to me, to connect with me. If she wanted, I would give her some soothing touch. Pearl looked at me for a moment, apparently considering my offer. Then she slowly approached me. Once close to me, Pearl stood with her head over the fence. I stood on her left side. Her eyes were soft and her head was relaxed. For a moment we simply stood together.

Glancing over my shoulder, I noted the others were focused on Bailey's shoeing session. Still with no horse of my own, I coveted any time I could connect with a horse and I relished this private time with Pearl, selfishly hoping that no one would notice what we were doing. I did not want them to think I was doing something weird with Pearl.

The others continued to focus on Bailey's shoeing session; their conversation, floating through the crisp autumn air, became a murmur in my background. The connection began to build between Pearl and me. Pearl relaxed more as her head dropped a few more inches, and she slowly blinked, her eyelids getting heavy. Before I placed my hands on Pearl, I silently asked her where she wanted to be touched and where I could help to release and ease her pain. Intuitively my left hand was drawn to the top of her head and my right to the side of her neck. I sensed that my hands did not need to be on her body. Instead, my hands settled into the space about five inches from her head. Once my hands were positioned, I felt a wave of pain move through my head. The pain felt tight, constricted, and an image of a blow to the head came to my mind. Flinching, I acknowledged the pain I felt as an empathetic response to Pearl's pain and that it was not mine, but energy wishing to pass through me. It subsided from my sensate experience. My attention then turned to my hands and Pearl's head.

Pearl's head had become more relaxed as it dropped lower and lower, the rest of her body still and unmoving. Her eyelids became heavier and started to droop. My hands followed, maintaining space between them and her head. Pearl began to relax, and I noticed the heat begin to move through my hands. Energy was moving and shifting. I was then intuitively drawn to place my hands around her jaw area, again a few inches away from her face. Once again I felt pain, sharp and metallic, in my own jaw. I invited her to let her pain go and communicated silently to her that no one was going to hurt her again. Heat began to return to my hands, moving through them again. Pearl was relaxing enough in her body for energy to be released from her through my hands. There we stood for some time together, with my hands offering comfort and my heart offering silent whispers of reassurance. My breathing matched hers, and time expanded.

I was unaware of the people around us. I was fully present and in the moment of sharing. Pearl too was completely present to the experience we were sharing. She was fully relaxed and trusted our connection. Her head dropped more, and my hands moved around her head and on her head in different positions, each time sensing movement of heat from my hands.

My heart began to ache for the horse's suffering. I continued to whisper comforting thoughts and sweet seeds of hope. Suddenly I felt a wave of energy and emotion pass through my body. I felt a deep resonance and empathetic connection with Pearl. Pearl stood, still and quiet. Two large tears welled up and fell from Pearl's left eye. Her eye was softly blinking, pinched with worry and sadness. My heart sunk as I empathized with the pain, abuse, and misfortune this horse must have experienced. Pearl's tears touched me deeply. I had never shared such an experience with a horse.

We were not alone. Curious eyes penetrated our sacred space. I looked up to see that the owner of the horse and my girlfriend Becky had been watching us. I asked them if they had seen Pearl's tears. They had. In that moment I disconnected and placed my attention with the others; Pearl's head came back up, her eyes larger and alert, and she pulled her head away from me.

Our moment of connection was gone. How vulnerable that moment had been. I had given her my complete attention. In the middle of our sacred moment, my attention had shifted from holding a soft safe space to communicating with my friends. I had moved from my heart to my head, instead of simply being with her, without distraction or judgment. Rather than totally trusting what my own eyes and heart had told me was true, my attention instead had turned for validation from the others.

Pearl, a horse who had been abused, had decided to approach me, had allowed my hands to be placed around her head, and then had released tears from her eyes. Once the sense of sacred space and safety was no longer present, she chose to break the bond with me. Pearl was at full choice to experience what she desired. I brought my full attention and focus back to her. Silently I asked her if she wanted to continue. She looked at me for a moment, and then she slowly turned and walked away. My heart sank as I realized our moment was complete and over.

The moment was gone, and it was because I had allowed my attention to go to my friends in the moment of Pearl's shedding of tears. I had shifted from my heart into my head. Pearl was complete with our experience, and our moment of connection was over. It may have only been five minutes total, but in those five minutes our connection had been strong. Through being fully present, energy and tears had been released. Pearl had found someone she thought could understand her pain and offer her comfort.

"Somewhere, somewhere

In time's own space

There must be some sweet pastured place

Where creeks sing on and tall trees grow

Some Paradise where horses go.

For by the love that guides my pen

I know great horses live again."

—Stanley Harrison

Hannah Lei

Hanna Lei is a beautiful 17-hand, bright red sorrel Thoroughbred. Her high withers give the impression she is even larger than she is. Before she arrived at a small ranch in Tucson, Arizona, she had been used for competitive hunter/jumper events. She was an expensive horse, with a wealthy owner who used her only for competitive jumping events, and little or no attention was given to her emotional needs.

Her owner's groom would prepare Hannah Lei, and then the owner would arrive, run her through the jumping course, and give her back to the groom. Hannah Lei's job was to do what she was asked—jump high and be fast. Hannah Lei, unfortunately, had a tragic accident. During a competition, she failed to clear a jump and fell over backwards, severely damaging her spine and hips. Never to be a hunter/jumper again, Hannah was of no further use to her owner. She was not even suitable as a school horse.

Luckily for Hannah, instead of the ill-fated path given to most horses deemed useless—sent to an auction and, if not purchased, loaded onto a trailer and transported to a slaughter house—she was donated to a small ranch where she could spend her time peacefully grazing or working with people in equine experience learning activities.

Like most Thoroughbreds, Hannah is a highly sensitive and responsive horse. Her large size is misleading; many people fear her and think her to be domineering; she is, however, a sweet, gentle mare with a very big heart. Beneath her physical presence is a horse who has suffered physically in the hands of humans but is still willing to connect with and work with them in a more nurturing and caring setting. Hannah is not free of her physical pain. When she moves around the pasture, her hind end sways awkwardly.

I spent two months at the ranch in Tucson. It was an uncommonly rainy and cool winter. When the sun did emerge, with it came a chorus of birds and the pungent fresh smell of the earthy creosote and desert brush. Next to the ranch, a river wash fluctuated in depth with the rain. Every morning and evening the coyotes would run through the wash yipping and crying, alerting every canine to protect its owner and property. Peaceful moments were interrupted with chaos and the chaos was restored by stillness. The river wash continued to rise and fall with torrents of rain followed by sun.

I had traveled to Tucson in search of a community that would understand the deep connection I felt with horses. Tucson was a hotbed for equine-based learning work, so I had moved there to study for a year to continue to grow and learn with the horses and to enhance my budding business of equine-based learning programs. My high hopes for deep connection were soon dashed. Tucson was a larger city than I was used to, and it was a challenge to find the community I desired in the city. The people in my program came and left. Similar to the cycle of the rain and coyotes, the fluctuation between activity and non-activity felt extreme. When my colleagues were in town there was plenty to do; when they left the quiet and stillness crept in. The ranch where I lived provided little activity, and as the winter holidays approached a heavy, wet energy hung like dense fog.

My morning meditations became integrated into my morning chore of mucking the pasture. This time was deemed personal and private time, and I treasured it deeply. Through sharing moments of silence and being present to the rhythm of nature with the horses, I felt a deeper connection to them. From the very beginning I felt a resonance and attraction to Hannah. She struck a chord deep within me, and I felt drawn to her. For many days I mucked around her, softly whispering invitations for her to connect with me. Her eyes followed me, and every so often her long legs would take steps toward me, but she always stopped a fair distance away.

One morning Hannah was sluggish, and I noticed she was favoring her back right leg. She had injured it a few days previously, and her owner had dismissed the problem as superficial. However, the wound was deeper than her owner had realized and had become infected. Hannah 's whole leg was swollen and stiff, causing her great discomfort.

As her owner called the vet, I stood with Hannah. She placed her head in the crook of my armpit, pressing her forehead into my shoulders. We stood for a half an hour, unmoving, her eyelids closed, her head against my body. I spoke soft words to her and matched my breath with hers. Her body warmed mine, and we melded together, her weight leaning into me. This gentle giant, vulnerable and exhausted, had sought me for comfort that day; she humbled me.

Our bond was interrupted when the vet arrived. Just one day after her treatment, Hannah's leg was on its way to healing. Our few moments of standing together had left me feeling connected to Hannah. I secretly felt thrilled that she had let me comfort her.

Mucking continued to be a favorite part of my day, a time when my mind was silent. When Hannah would stroll near, I left her free to do what she wanted. I never approached her, but instead allowed her the space to approach me. When she did, I rewarded her with gentle strokes on her long, strong neck.

The more I learned about horses, the more I began to approach less and wait more. I wanted their kinship on their terms and in their time. Each horse was invited to engage with me when the timing felt right. Each horse would come and go. I began to feel as if I were mingling within the herd versus being an outsider coming into the herd with a human perspective and agenda about something to achieve. The horses became my friends; with them I could find peace and solace.

Every day when I mucked, I practiced the Mind Body Method, a centering process I had developed in my Life Coaching practice. This process helped me to center myself in my body, scan the sensations I was feeling, and identify the emotional state I was holding. The practice pulled me from my busy thinking head into a deeper awareness of my self.

The more I was aware of every aspect of my being, the more often the horses would approach me. It didn't matter if I felt sad, mad, frustrated, happy, or peaceful. My process of going inward and using my own sensing abilities bridged a communication barrier between us. Once I began to interpret the world through my emotions instead of focusing strongly through my head, the horses became more relaxed. It was as if I was speaking their language, a communication based in feeling and not thinking. Each time I did this, we became more harmonious with each other.

Unfortunately, my time at the ranch was coming to an end. It had not always been a peaceful place for me to live. Sometimes the owner and I would find a natural easy connection; other times an underlying current of stress seemed to be present. The horses were my refuge from the human-based dynamics. It was difficult to leave when I felt such a strong sense of belonging with the horses. I dreaded the inevitable parting of our paths. They were my friends.

One day near the end of my stay, I was feeling rather emotional, yet not quite able to understand what I was feeling. My internal landscape was full of confusion and emotional turmoil. I moved around the pasture, pushing the wheelbarrow while silently telling the horses what I was sensing and experiencing in my body.

The horses had gathered together, eating their supper. Pausing for a moment, I stood still under a mesquite tree and focused on my breath to keep myself present. Hannah slowly raised her head; her eyes softly penetrated my heart. Moving away from the herd and her food, she walked directly toward me, her eyes never wavering. My body softened with an anticipation I could not define. Hannah and I had developed a trust in our relationship, and it was comforting to see her move her big, lanky body toward me. I welcomed her into my space. As she approached, I put my rake down and stood silently.

Hannah bent her neck and pushed her nose against my left knee. This knee has been injured repeatedly and often causes me pain. Not once but twice, her gentle nudging brought my awareness to my leg. I continued to stand relaxed with my hands at my side. Slowly her head moved up my body, pausing for a soft touch to my stomach. Hannah then lifted her head so that her head was level with mine, her large eye only about eight inches from my own. Her eye was a world unto itself; shades of blues and browns with twinkles of yellow surrounded an orbit of deep blue black. My spirit slipped into the world behind the glassy pool. Lost in the moment and the world I had discovered in her eye, I felt a release of sadness move through my body. My heart felt full and then stretched. The injustice of life surrounded my every thought as I looked at Hannah's body. I silently communicated my sorrow that she was in such pain and had experienced her accident. I knew in that moment that Hannah and I shared something beyond words, a clear understanding of each other.

The world I saw within her eye continued to pull me in as I questioned how anyone could ignore, misuse, or disrespect the essence of such a magnificent creature. A rising tide of tears sprung up through my heart and throat, and a familiar fuzzy sting burned behind my eyes.

I looked to Hannah, standing so close. Hannah's own eye, dark and warm, began to well up with fluid. A large pear-shaped tear collected in the corner or her eye and slid down her face, streaking her sorrel hair and then dropping to the ground and disappearing into the desert sand. There we stood, two sensitive beings sharing an understanding, our eyes remaining locked. Time stood still beneath the mesquite tree. Then, as soft as a spring breeze, my sadness softened and subsided.

Hannah's moist nose gently pressed against my stomach, and I brought all my awareness to that spot. I felt tightness and constriction. Without reaching out to touch or stroke Hannah, I spoke silently to her, telling her I felt her support and tenderness. I thanked her over and over for being a beautiful horse in physical appearance and in spirit. Together we stood until Hannah lifted her head and moved a few inches away from my body. Intuitively, this movement felt like a sign that she was complete in touching and connecting with me. Only then did I allow my hands to rise from the sides of my body. I began to stroke Hannah's neck and head, whispering sweet "Thank you's" and acknowledging her gentleness and caring. She stayed a few minutes for the comforting touch. Hannah then strolled away and went back to her meal.

Hannah gave me a moment of connection and complete circle of support. There was an unspoken understanding, an allowing of moments to simply be, and a deep resonance though my heart. There was a mutual shared empathy. She had helped me to release, and in that process I believe the experience helped her as well.

There is no question in my mind why women are attracted to horses. They are willing to be with us and to share the sensitive emotional states that simmer in our hearts and centers that we often find hard to share with our own human herd and its social structures. Emotional fears do not frighten horses away, nor does fear of emotions. They offer a refuge from an often callous and judgmental world.

It is only through the strength of knowing and understanding our own emotions and experiences that we can hold the space and truly be empathic for others. Deeper connections and bonding result from this process, and empathy builds a bridge of deep understanding that enhances trust.

There is an enormous amount of personal power in the ability to feel, understand, and express emotions. Emotions that bring forth tears or crying get a bad rap in our culture. This sort of emotion is viewed as irrational behavior, weak and undesirable. Many alternative health studies now claim that our emotions play an important role in our health. When emotions are held back, the energy of the body becomes stagnant and the natural flow of energy is interrupted. This condition contributes to *dis-ease.*

I coach individuals to learn how to listen to the emotions that rise up, to use those emotions as appropriate signs or messages, and to allow the energy of those emotions to be expressed at appropriate times in appropriate ways. Allowing emotions and gaining emotional strength and agility leads one to a less emotionally driven or reactive state of being. Instead, a higher level of consciousness emerges, and multi-levels of self-awareness and integration are achieved. People who become highly adept at listening to and working with their emotions become powerful individuals. They are attuned to listen to the first signs, to pick up inklings, before they reach the more amplified emotional state.

This is the teaching that horses can offer humans. Horses always sense energy around them; their survival depends on it. They process such information through awareness of sensations in their bodies, and they assess their situation and respond accordingly. Instinctive beings that are preyed upon, horses must be ready for an acute fight-or-flight response to any potentially threatening situation.

Just as I had offered a nonjudgmental space allowing Pearl to soften and release in my presence, Hannah provided the same for me. Her soft manner and grounding energy, along with the deep haunting pool within her eye, took me to a place that allowed my mixed emotions to emerge and transcend. Simultaneously, I experienced empathy for her situation and the pain that she had suffered. Together this mutual understanding and resonance, experienced on a sensory level, created a space for both of us to release tears that were being held within.

To me, the tender, caring connection between horses and humans—different species without a common spoken language—confirms what many people seek to believe: that there is an invisible force that connects every living thing in the world, a language without words, a shared understanding and knowing. When we can pause and breathe in the moment, tune back into our senses, and be fully present with another being, these moments come and embrace us, removing the barriers of our false sense of separateness.

Six months after moving away from Tucson, I was still thinking about Hannah. Images of her big beautiful eyes and sorrel coat kept popping into my mind. A voice deep within me said it was time to write about her. Trusting my inner guidance, I sat down and began to write. Even when writing about her, deep tears welled up, and my heart felt full again. How was it that she could continue to touch my heart when she was thousands of miles away? When I completed my writing, I felt a deep sense of completion at honoring this lovely, long-legged sorrel.

A day later, Hannah's owner contacted me. The previous day, the day I finished my writing, Hannah had colicked and died. As Hannah was taking flight, leaving her earthly physical existence for her spiritual origins, my hand and pen had flown across paper; my heart felt a need to capture and honor the sweetness and essence of her being.

She had lived a tough life, where others—unaware, careless, and selfish in their actions—used her for their own benefit. Her days of competition had not brought her joy and pride in serving, but pain and suffering. During her last years she had found a quiet home, where her owner gave her space to simply be.

The horse is not here for humans to do with as we please. We should be humbled by the horse's willingness to partner and to serve, to allow a smaller predatory animal on its back. We owe horses appreciation and tribute for their nobility. We must remember our time with them is a privilege and an honor that *they* give to us, not something we should take for granted.

Years ago horses ploughed fields, delivered mail, and carried soldiers to battle. Horses can now offer a new way to serve, by asserting themselves and asking to be equal partners with humans by challenging humans to look beyond current accepted assumptions about the purpose of a horse. No longer willing to go at the pace of man, the horse can teach us to return to our roots, the ones that are deeply connected to the earth. The horse keeps its power each day it decides to keep its nature and connection to what keeps it in harmony and peace. Each time the horse speaks, we must listen. We must learn new approaches to work, with kindness and in partnership, in a way that honors the horse as the sentient being it is.

Horses offer humans the wisdom of knowing one's heart and the understanding that all beings are created equal. Through each act of kindness and every desire to understand rather than control, the human can make a difference.

My truth knows that horses feel. They feel agitation and competition when a bachelor challenges another stallion. They feel harmony and peace when they are doing what they do best: grazing and moving about on the land. They stand tall and show pride when they have served and contributed and are respected. They become frustrated with human mental nonsense and experience loss from being separated from their mates. They become dull and despondent when their spirit is not recognized and honored. All of this happens when they are in the hands of man. That is when horses cry.

"Come on people now, smile on your brother, everybody get together, try to love one another right now."
—"Get Together," Chester Williams Powers, Jr.

Come Together

It was early May in the Rocky Mountains of Colorado, a risky time for an equine workshop because weather conditions can change dramatically and quickly. Luckily the weather blessed us for this workshop. Little did I know of all the other blessings I would receive throughout the weekend.

The workshop site was a hundred-year-old homestead. The run-down ranch house sat in a scooped out meadow, with juniper pines on one hillside and high alpine sage on the other. The small house was the essence of the old West, its wood siding weathered and worn. A creek big enough to make itself heard but not always seen ran though the meadow. Mother Nature had created a sacred space, a place that felt protected from the rest of the world.

My host and the owner of the ranch, Susan, had grown up in Wyoming. Susan had been raised with the traditional Western ranching approach and philosophy about horses. The no-nonsense approach had served her well and helped her get by for a long time. Her many years of experience included horse births and deaths, accidents and sales. She had seen it all. Her heart yearned for more. It was time to explore what was beyond the eyes, ears, and senses, beyond logic and practicality. She dared to venture into unknown waters, trusting her intuition and following her desire to create a deeper connection with her herd of horses. She was on a spiritual path of growth.

Susan's aunt Anne was just in from the East Coast and was excited to explore possibilities through learning the wisdom of the horse. Not nearly the seasoned horsewoman her niece was, Anne had experienced the power of learning with horses with a previous facilitator. Anne brought thirty years as a trained psychotherapist and sixty-one years of life experience. These two women had experienced trauma emotionally and physically through divorce, horse accidents—including broken backs—alcoholism, and rape.

Each woman was primed for the weekend adventure, smiling and excited. However, logistical challenges before the workshop rang a warning bell. My host's last-minute unavailability to help with any of the set-up contributed to uneasy feelings.

The first morning of the workshop I practiced what I teach; I found myself shoveling two-foot-high weeds and grass out of the round pen. I had not visited the premises thoroughly enough before the workshop. A hard look at the graveled round pen confirmed that my attempts were futile. I worked as fast and as furiously as I could to remove the tallest of the weeds from the center so that at least the inside of the pen would appear clean. There was no way I could clear the outer edges in the time I had left.

A horse in this round pen would easily find tidbits to graze on during a session, a challenge and a significant distraction for the horse. As tension began to build inside me, I centered myself by taking a deep breath and then asked, "What wants to happen?" and "What is most important in this moment?" Perfection was not appropriate now. Resistance never produces good results and is taxing energetically. Flow needed to happen, and the only way to achieve that was to drop my agenda. A horse that chose to eat grass during a session would serve the learning for that client. Ignoring all remaining grass clumps and scattered manure, I turned my attention to preparing the horses. Soon crunching on the gravel indicated the arrival of the first client.

Seldom will a group of women join together and immediately form a circle of support, connection, and cohesiveness; this group did so with complete ease. Some of the women already knew each other. All knew or had met Susan. Each came with her unique challenges, traumas, and desires. Some had past experiences with horses, others did not. Susan had brought together a heart-centered group of women with a high potential for learning and healing.

After greetings and a morning lecture, everyone milled around the paddocks to meet the horses. Shortly afterward the round pen sessions began. During the first session, Shadow, the horse in the round pen, seemed less interested in grazing on the ripe, sweet blades of grass than I had imagined. It was a relief.

Susan's aunt Anne was the second round pen session participant of the day. Anne stood outside the round pen, and we began to check in with her body and her emotional information. I coached Anne to bring her attention to the areas of her body that she was most noticing.

Clients are often drawn to areas such as their heart, throat, lower belly, back, or solar plexus. Once a client's attention is focused on a specific area, she continues to explore the sensations, emotions, and/or messages that come from that part of her body. This process provides the client an opportunity to become still and listen deeply to her body wisdom. This deep, focused listening is called the Mind Body Method.

The horse that Anne selected to work with, Cajun, now in the round pen, was anything but interested in what we were doing. His white Appaloosa coat splattered wildly with red spots, black-freckled head, and eyes contradicted his unassuming presence. Cajun stretched his neck and contorted his body to reach under and through the bottom tier of the round pen to get to the greener grass on the other side.

As a client moves through the Mind Body Method, the horse responds at key times by moving closer. These are the times when a client gets in touch with the energy and sensations rising in her body as she becomes more centered in her awareness and present in the moment. The more congruent and "in the body" the client becomes, generally the closer the horse moves. Often, as soon as the client moves away from her body and heart and back to her analyzing mind, the horse will promptly move away. In this way the horse becomes a monitor and indicator of the human's awareness level, the ability to listen and be centered in their body.

We remained outside of the round pen as I coached Anne, and she struggled with staying in her body. She would locate an area that was speaking to her, but staying with the sensations arising in her body was taxing. Each time she found a spot in her body and began to center and focus her attention, she would tell me the stories of her life, moving her awareness from her body to the safety of her head. Back and forth we went from story (head) to body, body to story (head). The energy from her voice also seemed to be coming from the top of her body, from her head. Her shallow breath produced a voice just above a whisper. The pitch, slightly higher than normal, sounded fake; her voice lacked authenticity and depth. Part of the real Anne was not present in the tone and tenor of her voice.

Cajun watched us from the corner of his eye but wasted no time with us. He continued to munch on sweet grass around the pen's outer edges. Doubts crept into my mind as I saw the dynamics playing out. What if Cajun continued to eat for the duration of the session, completely ignoring Anne?

As facilitator, it is important that I control my overriding voice of fear whenever it emerges. This voice creates a disconnection from trusting the flow of the process. When this voice "speaks," I become attached to what might *not* happen, or what unusual, unexpected, or unbalanced event might happen. It brings the urge to manipulate and to control. The beauty of working with the horses is that it is not the facilitator's job to control outcome, manipulate experiences, or become goal-oriented. Instead, the facilitator holds a space that allows the horse and human to work together to create their own dynamic, often only weaving in small comments and questions for guidance. As a result, sometimes something beyond and much greater than what the human ego can create transpires naturally in the session.

Still outside the pen, Anne turned to face her horse. I continued to coach her through the Mind Body Method process, and she scanned through her body, checking in with key areas that drew her attention. Often these areas hold important messages that are waiting to emerge. Her throat and lower belly were very alive with sensation. She identified her sensations as contracted and tight, controlling and limiting, and she was experiencing fear. Still, Cajun gave no sign of connecting or responding to her findings by moving closer. After completing the body scanning process, Anne moved her awareness to her heart. She then expressed her heart's desire or intention for the session. Anne's intention was to experience being with Cajun, to create a connection, and to have him look her directly in the eye. As she articulated her heart-centered intention, Cajun continued to appear disinterested. Anne and I talked about safety and her comfort level with Cajun. She was ready to enter the round pen and to experience her heart's desire.

Cajun did not react or respond as Anne stepped inside the round pen. However, he did keep one eye on Anne. He continued to meander around the round pen with his head down, eating, appearing unconcerned. Tentatively, Anne followed him. As they weaved toward and away from each other, Anne was trying to connect with Cajun and draw him to her. Cajun was clearly searching for the next delicious tiny blade or morsel.

The inner voice of fear and doubt jumped into my mind. "Where is this session going to go? Would the client receive anything from this horse?" I continued to breathe deeply and slowly in order to re-center myself, fighting my mind and ego's urge to interfere, to ask questions and to "create" a successful experience for my client. With effort I pushed my negative thoughts away and replaced them with trusting the process and being fully present in the moment.

Within a few minutes Anne looked over at me and declared, "He's not going to look at me or come to me." Tears streamed down her face; she seemed to shrink and crumble as her body hunched over, and she walked to the edge of the round pen, defeated. She looked childlike and vulnerable, a living memory of being rejected on the playground. Cajun walked away, seeking more green grass.

Once again Anne checked in with her body and focused on the area that she most noticed, the area that wanted attention. Her hand went to her throat. She identified tight, constricted sensations, a sense of not being able to speak. Hoarsely, she spoke of a time in her life when she had broken her back and then, in halting, stumbling syllables, when she was gang-raped. She had been frozen then, unable to move physically or to scream out. No matter how hard she had tried, she was unable to call out for help during that traumatic event. Her body froze as she endured the violation.

Her hands visibly shook, and her face was flushed with red. I asked her, "What wants to speak through your throat? What needs to be said?" Anne immediately replied, "Help, but I can't get it out." "Speak it," I coached her. A timid "help" passed between her lips. "Again. Say it again. And louder this time," I coached her. Four times she spoke her cry for help. Each time it became a bit louder. Yet I knew it was not the only thing that was being held in her throat; something more sought freedom and release and wanted to come forth.

Then, out of context, Anne said, "I used to sing. Oh, how I used to love to sing. I sang for a sixties rock band." Tears poured from her eyes.

"What was your favorite song to sing?" I asked her.

Softly came a stutter, a deep swallow, and then with hesitation Anne recited, "Come on people now, smile on your brother, everybody get together, try to love one another right now."

Cajun continued grazing, with one eye on us, a longer glance than usual, though he remained aloof to our presence. I wondered if he would be any part of the session.

"Let's hear you sing it," I coached Anne, "Come on, sing it! You can do it."

Her voice was harsh and crackly, raspy at best. As soon as she sang, there was a slight movement from Cajun's ears, his eye now fully on us as he continued to graze. Anne's eyes were glued on me and pleaded for more encouragement. "Again," I said. "Louder, let's really hear it."

Anne's next attempt came from a deeper place in her chest. This time there was rhythm and tone. Her body lifted, her eyes became bright, as she stared directly at me. "One more time, Anne. You can do it. Do it!"

Anne took a deep breath all the way into her belly. A voice of power, passion, and depth emerged—a voice I had not heard before. The lyrics came to life as she sang with every fiber of her body. "Come on people now, smile on your brother, everybody get together, try to love one another right now." A wave of energy surged through me. The ring of Anne's last note flowed far beyond the borders of the round pen and settled into silence.

Cajun's head popped up, and he moved straight across the round pen to Anne's side. He softly placed his nose to her throat and then to her heart, breathing deeply in each spot.

"He came to me! Did you see that? Cajun came to me!" Anne's childlike glee spilled over with joy and excitement, her eyes bright and shiny. We continued to stand together, the three of us. Cajun stood, silently breathing, while Anne focused on reconnecting with her body. She felt new, different sensations in her throat and her body. The pain of her past had been washed away, and she had reclaimed a piece of her joy. The energy in her throat had moved with the song, and the energy in her belly had dissipated.

Once her learning was fully integrated, I encouraged Anne to take a minute to say thank you to her four-legged teacher. Anne turned to look at Cajun. No longer grazing or even interested in grazing, Cajun had followed along a few steps behind her. As Anne turned and looked at him, he took two steps toward her and raised his head so he could gaze directly into her eyes. Their eyes locked together in stillness. Anne's tears flowed again as her heart's desire was completely fulfilled by Cajun. Together they stood, gazing deeply into each other's eyes and souls. Anne's willingness to risk, to speak up, to find her authentic voice had created a moment of sharing and connection with Cajun. They had come together.

Anne, I, and all of the other participants remained in silence, feeling the expansion of time and the heightening awareness of our senses. No words could express the awe of witnessing Anne's shift from victim into the essence and spirit of her authentic self through interacting with Cajun. Cajun was simply being a horse and responding to the quality of her energy.

As the facilitator, I could not have planned for this process and learning to unfold. I could not have manipulated the horse to respond in the way he did. It would not have served my client if I had tried to make things "right" or to tried to control how the session played out. The grazing, my biggest fear, turned into an asset for the sessions. My ability to remove my ego from controlling the learning environment and willingness to move into full trust and acceptance of what could naturally emerge contributed to the success of the session. This session was based on the philosophy of allowing what wants to happen to come forth.

In Peter Levine's book *Waking the Tiger: Healing Trauma*, he writes about how trauma can become trapped in the body. During a traumatic event, instead of a fight or flight response, the body freezes and the person disassociates from the experience. Disassociation is the body's natural coping mechanism. This survival mechanism guarantees that a person in imminent danger or facing death will not feel the pain of the injury or death. The nervous system and the brain has disconnected from what is happening in the body.

When death does not happen, the memory of the trauma becomes locked in the cells of the body, burying the experience from the conscious mind. Then, when a circumstance arises that appears to the mind or body to be similar, the body responds the same way. It disassociates. Until the person becomes aware of this sensory arousal and takes a different action during this highly stimulating moment, the cycle of the original trauma continues.

Anne broke the cycle of victimhood by finding her voice with Cajun. Instead of shrinking back into the victim pattern, she remained fully present in her body and in the moment and, with coaching, released the word "help." Several times she said "help," each time establishing a new pathway of response in her brain and nervous system to the old trauma. Then she recovered her lost singing voice by singing her favorite lyric out loud until power and authenticity were behind her words. She came fully into herself, her powerful, authentic self. In that moment, Anne broke the pattern of being a victim. Anne processed the negativity out of her body—the pain from her trauma; her projections of the fear that others would not be there for her or would ignore her needs. She reclaimed her authenticity through her voice as it rose from deep within her belly.

Cajun responded to the release of the old energy. Once she became fully present in her body, found her voice, and remained fully in her body, he came directly to her. Horses have little desire to be physically close to individuals who are not in their body. Horses' primary way of communicating with each other is through their bodies and what they sense and feel in the environment. Their ability to be in tune and in harmony enhances their comfort level and survival in the herd. A horse that cannot clearly draw cues from his environment is a handicap to the herd. A human who cannot fully sense their personal internal environment would also be a handicap to the herd and, therefore, is rejected by the herd.

Horses teach humans a body-centered awareness, their most natural approach to life. Horses are naturally embodied, until a fear penetrates and leads them to a fight or flight response. While in a relaxed, safe state, a horse's large presence creates an energy field that helps to ground a person focused on doing so within his or her own body. This act of becoming fully aware of one's self is the first step to removing the stress and tension that we unconsciously carry. In becoming present and able to allow what is uncomfortable, a person experiences a moment in time when the answer and the solution will naturally emerge from a deeper place of inner wisdom.

Humans tend to *do* too much. We chase life. We try to control others and circumstances so we can feel safe, content, and happy inside. If you watch horses, you will notice that they, for the most part, do little and spend much time grazing and dozing.

Horses live in a powerful, authentic state of being. They are naturally connected to their source within the animal world and to elements around them. They do not experience the internal struggles of ego, attachment, and agenda that pull humans off course. The horse will always respond positively to the truth when it emerges from a client, because once the truth is spoken, an immediate relaxation comes over the human body. The horse is appreciative because he or she can return to grazing, in harmony with their natural state of being.

Many equine experiential programs focus on things to do with horses. Then, when the client cannot successfully achieve the objective—the thing they are trying to accomplish through the activity—the behavior that preceded the incident is explored. The client examines his actions. This can be effective for learning, and often the horse is used as a tool in this process. Everyone waits for the moment the human fails so there can be something to process. The focus is on waiting for something to go wrong. The horse is there as part of the plan, with little appreciation shown for the essence and nature that the horse offers.

The true gift from the horse is an understanding of the nature of the horse. To understand and to know the horse and to explore a relationship with the horse through that understanding provides a level of learning that is based on mutual respect and honor. Horses are much more sophisticated creatures than many give them credit for. The primary teaching that horses have to offer humans is the art of being present. Whether introverted or extroverted, horses are completely present in the moment and, through their body language, express exactly what they are experiencing.

My programs are designed so the potential of my clients can emerge through their relationships with the horse. As I coach them to become more present in the moment, to speak the language of the horse, I am also coaching them to access their authentic nature and power. I do not teach them to displace or project their pain and emotions onto the horse; I teach them to own and feel it for themselves, often for the first time in their lives. In doing so they naturally discover a part of themselves that has been lost in the harshness of the world and their experiences. The horse, always at liberty, moves and engages with the client in a manner that no human could design. In my equine-based learning sessions, by holding the intention and focusing on what is *possible,* hearts are opened by the horses.

Only by being present can one's ability to distinguish between fear-based states of being and authentic states of expression be achieved. Each time the client reaches the authentic state of expression, a part of them is returned to themselves. The only time a human experiences true power, the power that is based in authenticity, is when a human is body-centered and present in the moment, free of the ego and connected to their higher wisdom. Horses are seen as powerful creatures because this is their natural state of being. They are always in the moment: ego-less, body-centered, and ultimately focused on achieving a cooperative society in their herd.

Anne never actually tried to do anything with Cajun. She didn't try to make him move around the round pen, lungeing and exercising him. She did not force her will upon him. What Anne did was bravely open her heart to *being* with him fully, allowing her limiting subconscious aspects to be released. Then she found herself, the truth of her voice, the song that rang true in her heart, and only then could she also find a willing and open partner in Cajun. From that place of authenticity, he was ready to connect and then follow her. He had blessed us all through mirroring Anne's inner self. Through being who she was, in her pain and her brightness, she found herself an equine partner.

"When bestride him, I soar, I am a hawk; he trots the air; the earth sings when he touches it; the basest horn of his hoof is more musical than the pipe of Hermes."

—William Shakespeare, *Henry V*

The Fullness of Moon

One of the most important aspects of any partnership is the right partner. Whether in business, love, athletic adventures, traveling, the chemistry of two beings coming together to make a whole creates something greater than the individual parts. The same is true with horses.

Coming back to horses was an enjoyable experience while I was working with Hope. She had picked me and wanted a partner. She was bright and smart, and I was eager and willing. She always waited for me at the gate when I arrived, and she followed me around wherever I walked. She and I did well together when I was in the saddle. My intentions would translate to her, and we moved easily into transitions or around obstacles. She had me hooked on horses again. Our connection flowed like water.

After working with Hope, I traveled and facilitated equine-based learning programs for several years at many barns in the United States and Canada. During this process I was exposed to a tremendous number of horses and owners. Each barn had its own level of consciousness about the treatment of and relationship to horses. At some barns I felt frustrated over the mistreatment of horses and replaced it with hope that the concepts taught in my programs would have a positive effect. Traveling proved to be very educational for me.

I also continued to seek horses to partner with for my own growth. Finding horses that needed attention was not a challenge; there are an ample number of horses with busy owners. Flash, Hannah Lei, Hope, and many more not mentioned in these pages have graced me with their presence and kinship and stretched my horsemanship skills. However, finding the *right* horse partner, one with good chemistry, became a challenge.

I did well in my groundwork, easily moving horses without a lead line through transitions, circling, backing, and stopping, all through connection, intention, and the pure enjoyment of dancing, with the energy between us our means of communication.

The shift into riding did not come as easily. The flow and the joy I felt on the ground would often diminish when I rode. None of the horses offered the same level of safety and trust that I had experienced with Hope. At some point I got scared. My lower body and hips would stiffen and my gut start to flutter. The horse would react to my energy, and a downward spiral of frustration and fear would create disconnection between the horse and me. I felt I had to become a better horsewoman to be respected by clients and colleagues. The task felt daunting.

After many horses and attempts, I finally saw what I was doing wrong. First, in my desire to ride, I took any horse that was offered to me. I was not smart or clear about the best type, breed, sex, or personality that would help me move through my blocks.

Second, I had been using equipment that had been lent to me. One month I rode in a buttery leather English saddle, the next month I found myself in an old military McClellan saddle, and other times I rode in heavy Western gear. The exposure was educational, but the results were undesirable.

Third, I lacked consistent help or lessons from one person. I took series of lessons from many people, but I seldom felt that I made any progress or got beyond what one would learn in the first few lessons. Every time I started to get into a groove, either the horse would become unavailable or I moved to a new location. Consistency became an increasingly serious issue.

Things turned around when I decided to move to the Roaring Fork Valley in Colorado, where I had wanted to live since I was twenty years old. I relaxed into my home, a place where the land resonated with my heart and spirit. Finally, the nervous, unsettling feeling inside me switched off.

Shortly after moving to Colorado, I once again found myself back in Tucson for a visit. During dinner with colleagues, one person mentioned a buckskin Quarter Horse in Cimarron, New Mexico, who was ready for a new home. She thought he would be the perfect first horse for me. After years without a horse, my mind created an internal debate: Was I ready? . . . Why not? . . . Where would I put him? . . . What if I failed? I hesitated, until another woman at the table said she would be happy to take the horse. She knew its Quarter Horse bloodlines and the ranch where it was raised. There was no way I was going to lose a chance to have a horse, as I had with Hope. I called the owner that night and made arrangements to visit with the horse on my drive back to Colorado.

Three days later, beginning when I was about twenty miles from the ranch, the image of the buckskin's face began to appear in my mind. How beautiful he was: big, soft eyes, white and cream markings on his face, the tips of his ears outlined in black. He felt warm and comforting to my heart, like an old soul.

While I drove, I connected to him through my heart. I asked him to show me several things to confirm that he was the horse for me. He would need to come to the gate as soon as he saw me, without having to be fetched. He would join up with me quickly and easily and move with ease on the ground, doing what I asked without a lead line. I also wanted to see him lick and chew as we got to know each other. Finally, I asked him to watch me from the gate as I left instead of immediately returning to his herd.

The 200,000-acre ranch was clean, simple, and well-kept. An older homestead, white and trimmed in red, along with several outbuildings nestled among the cottonwoods. The compound sat close to a riverbed and was surrounded by vast open pastures that offered an enormous sense of expanse.

The woman who showed me the horse walked me to the barn. She suggested we grab a few treats, as the horse was a bit hard to catch. I almost asked for us not to, but I decided to keep my mouth shut.

As soon as we came into view, the horse looked up and began to walk directly to the gate. He was a beauty, an impressive 16.2 hands high, with a massive chest. Dapples covered his whole body, and his black mane and tail made a striking contrast. His registered name was Flashy Doc Warrior; his nickname, Moon, evoked the pale yellow color of the New Mexico full moon. As he came closer, I saw that his face was the spitting image of the horse in my mind an hour earlier—no surprise to me.

I spent time alone with Moon. We flowed together in a soft gentle dance. Moon's body exuded strength as he circled and moved through the transitions I asked for. He did everything that I had imagined us doing.

Moon had been bred and raised as a ranch horse. Pasture lands and mountain trails were normal country for his travels. In the last few years he had shown difficulty at the canter. Chiropractic adjustments helped, but it was not practical for a big ranching operation to haul a horse two hours each way for a treatment every week.

The typical policy for purchasing a horse is to hire a veterinarian to check the animal's health and to ride the horse to feel his strides or gaits. Disregarding advice from other horse owners, I instead followed my gut and heart, and the agreement was made. Without even riding Moon, I agreed to take the horse that had difficulty cantering. It seemed like a good fit at the time, and it proved to be just that.

Moon moved to Colorado about eight months later, after the winter storms had passed through. Leaving the ranch where he had been born and raised was not an easy transition. By the time he arrived in Colorado he had lost weight and was infested with ticks. His coat was missing the luster of good health that I had seen the previous fall. In the public barn where I had arranged for my programs to be held, Moon's paddock space was much smaller than he was accustomed to. His energy was low, and the other geldings picked on him. The once-dominant horse was at the bottom of the pecking order. He did not have the strength or desire to jostle and compete for a higher position. He was always last to have his pile of hay.

The barn provided a wonderful community of open and supportive people. The responsibility and the choices for Moon's care overwhelmed me. There were so many opinions and options to consider that it was hard to know what was right. Well-meaning people helped me the best they could, although I felt pressure to get up to the level of everyone else, as I had always been quick to learn new sports and activities. A month later Moon was riding in new gear, in new territory, and with a rider that lacked the level of skill he was accustomed to. We did okay, but in my heart I knew that it was wrong to push my agenda onto him (pushing and being unaware were the reasons I had been thrown and dragged years before). I wrestled with my ego and my sense of failure, and I finally let go of my desire to become a good rider.

Soon thereafter I facilitated a week-long equine learning program; several participants joined me for six days of highly hands-on work with horses. Moon proved to be generous in his nature and energy, to the point that I realized I was asking too much of him. In the middle of the program, a vet had to be called in for Moon.

A woman in one of my equine programs offered to move Moon to her pasture, where I could also hold my programs. Her herd of Paso Finos had participated in my previous program, and she was drawn to the work I was doing. Moon moved from the public barn. I traded all of the human support there for a large pasture that provided ample room for him to move around and graze without being picked on. I made the decision to move Moon with his health in mind. He would find his spot in the new herd, which was far more important than my desire to be a better rider. The priorities now were his health, the development of our relationship, and having him teach in my programs. Riding was last.

In the end it was the best thing for Moon. All summer he grazed in wide-open spaces similar to what he had been used to. We spent many hours together, often doing very little. The original headgear he had come with was shipped back to New Mexico, and I opted for a rope halter. The saddle that I had previously purchased was put into the closet, and instead I focused on riding him bareback.

Returning to bareback riding was the best thing I could have done. It was safe and easy, and getting ready was uncomplicated. If I fell off, there were no stirrups to catch my feet. As a child, I had the privilege of having my own balance beam to practice gymnastics. The dismounts I learned then easily translated into learning how to dismount a horse. I was used to performing a cartwheel or a jump off the balance beam and landing solidly with two feet on the ground.

I practiced emergency dismounts with Moon by bending my body forward and wrapping my arms around his neck. My legs naturally swung to one side of his back and then landed on the ground. His forward movement created just enough momentum for my body to naturally flow through the dismount at a walk and trot. I also practiced several different reins cues in conjunction with a quick exhale of my breath and a drop in the energy and movement of my body as a signal to stop.

Moon and I moved around the other horses in the pasture. Each day I learned about how to allow my body to meld to his and how to trust him. We moved from walking to a slow jog trot and then to an extended fast trot (we both avoided the canter). We opened gates, crossed bridges, stepped over logs. I climbed on the rails of an old wood fence to mount Moon. He positioned his barrel next to me, and I hoisted my body onto his high back. The more I behaved like a teenager with her first horse, the more joy I felt.

Each day Moon showed me when my confidence was lacking or when my mind drifted. He would stop in his tracks when I was not "present." Not until I returned my awareness to my breath and checked back into my body would he continue. I could have been forceful with my legs, giving stronger cues and asserting more power to make him go. I could have shown him who was the "boss," but I knew I wasn't yet, so I did not let my ego override my internal wisdom. I knew that

Moon was smarter than me and that I needed to learn more about him and his ways before assuming a leadership position. Curiosity was my motto, and I sought to hear what he communicated to me. I made a commitment to Moon that we would grow to know each other and as a team develop my leadership.

One day Moon tested my ability to listen to him. The Colorado Rockies are known for their afternoon thundershowers. The clouds can move quickly, and before you know it lightning is overhead. It was late August, and there were several bleak clouds on the ridge above the red rock hills surrounding the pasture. I chose to ignore them. Moon did not. About a hundred yards out into the field he stopped, turned his head, and shook his nose up and down in the direction of the barn. I redirected him back to the open field. We continued this dance a few times until Moon finally planted his feet and would not budge. Asserting myself, I tapped him with my legs, which made his belly shake, but his feet did not move. He was not fearful nor was he simply being difficult; he was being firm. He knew something I did not, and I thought it best to listen. We swung around and headed back to an old three-sided wood structure with a roof that provided the horses with protection from the elements. Walking more briskly than usual, we arrived at the shed, where I dismounted. Together we sought shelter under the shed's old planks, standing side by side as we watched the storm move quickly toward us. Lightning cracked, and the rain broke free of the black clouds that canopied over our heads. Waves of rain moved through the pasture and over our heads, and raindrops trickled down through the cracks of the loafing shed. Twenty minutes later the sun was shining again. We walked to the fence, and Moon stood still as I climbed up and onto his massive back. We then turned and headed back to the field to enjoy a lovely dry afternoon ride.

Some may criticize my decision to give my horse free rein that day, while others may understand. We walk a fine line between companionship and leadership with horses. Your horse wants you to be the leader and wants your confidence. Nonconforming behavior might be interpreted as though the horse is being difficult, stubborn, and agitated for no good reason. Everything depends on the horse and the situation: usually there is good reason. Even if a horse is fearful of something as simple as a flag or as harmless as a piece of paper or a line, respecting that fear allows the rider to work from a place of understanding.

Moon continually teaches me about the fine lines in the relationship between horse and human. His greatest gift is continuous patience as I develop into a better rider. A summer spent riding bareback increased my confidence and my understanding of his natural triggers and how I responded when he behaved in a nonconforming manner. There were times of challenge when I learned to assert myself and make firm requests to him to move beyond his fear. There were other times that it behooved me to listen to him.

Our time together without others watching and advising allowed Moon and me to discover each other without the pressure to perform. It helped me to release the energy patterns of old trauma and tension lodged deep within me from having been dragged, a gradual process that included moments of fear, frustration, impatience, and anger.

The first time I cantered on Moon, I did so bareback. Once I moved past this block, at my own pace and feeling completely safe and bonded with my horse, I had more confidence and motivation to become the better rider to which I aspired. Eventually I began to ride in a saddle, which for me was scarier than riding bareback. The stirrups made me nervous.

Everything about Moon's life had changed. Although he was no longer running cattle, when cows in the far field came near Moon's pasture, he lifted his head high, alert—he was ready to move! But now he had to adjust to a new owner, herd companions, and environment. Several months of relaxation and light exercise gave him time to sink into his new home and to learn his new job as a teacher for humans. Moon began to facilitate humans in equine coaching sessions. Instead of focusing on cattle, he learned how to focus on humans, giving them his full attention. His ability to work with people came instantly, and he proved to be quite good at his new line of service. His deep soul and massive and gentle body provided clients a safe space for their process.

Throughout the summer Moon received chiropractic sessions. His diet was adjusted to include feed supplements; additional supplements and herbs supported his immune system and general health. His shoes came off so his bare feet could touch the earth again.

After a long, restful summer, the snow fell early. My heart felt lonely, and I missed the community at the barn where we had started, so we moved back.

I purchased a Bob Marshall saddle that had much of what a regular saddle offered but at a quarter of the weight. The saddle was treeless, so the internal structure of the saddle flexed with the body of the horse. Moon moved beneath me much like when we were bareback.

Patience had never been my forte. I had always rushed forward with any new sport or activity that had struck my fancy. I dove into projects, rushed into relationships, and made rash decisions, all in the attempt to avoid the foundational work needed to build and support a new project, relationship, or endeavor. Moon taught me to slow down and be more consistent. When I hurried forward, I always ended up coming back to fix things that I did not do well. He refused to lift his hoof for cleaning when my breath was shallow or my mind was distracted. When I was not fully present to my environment and to my body, he let me know.

In his book *A Good Horse is Never a Bad Color*, Mark Rashid tells a tale about true patience in working with a horse that has nervous energy and does not trust humans. In the chapter "A Good Start," the trainer focuses on taking small steps and offering lots of space and respect for the horse, which allows the horse to move into the relationship at his own pace. This process involved weeks of consistent care and slow interactions between human and horse. It took months to build trust in the open fields and a few years for the once flighty, distrustful horse to become a consistent, reliable companion.

Just as a horse needs time to put all the pieces together to trust his or her owner, a rider often needs the same. The beginning of my relationship with Moon was not about me training Moon. It was just the opposite. I was the skittish human who did not trust the horse. Even with a calm, gentle, and well-trained horse, my internal alarm system went off at the slightest sign of physical risk. (Moon is a big horse, and it was a long way down to the ground.) Our small steps toward partnership empowered me to be a better, and calmer, human for him.

Through our partnership, something beyond each of us has been created. Nothing in the world is worth doing alone. My life has become whole through the fullness of my partnership with Moon.

"There is no secret so close as that between a rider and his horse."

—R. S. Surtees

At times I encourage individuals, if they feel inspired, to write a poem or story or create a piece of art that expresses their learning and insights with the horses. The reflection required in the artistic process brings the individual into a deeper level of awareness and meaning of their experience. Many find long forgotten and hidden talents and others discover their creative expression as they work with words, paper, colors, and shapes.

Below is the story "Lay Down By My Side," written by Connie Harvey, a young woman who offered to share her insights about her equine experience.

Lay Down by My Side

by Connie Harvey

I really wasn't sure what to expect from the workshop before arriving. I thought that it would be an introduction to Equine Facilitated Learning and coaching and how the processes work, but I did not expect to have a powerful personal experience that completely moved me in a way I never thought possible.

The first exercise of the workshop was about meeting and connecting with the horses. It challenged me to move outside of myself, outside of my comfort zone. I had to trust myself and listen to my inner voice. It was during this exercise that I first had contact with Reggie. As I stood just outside his stall, I noticed that Reggie stood at the back of his stall with his rear end facing the door. He didn't seem to be interested in participating in the activity, unlike the other horses that were eager to engage with the participants; they stood with their heads reaching across the stall panels. It wasn't until I walked away from Reggie's stall that he turned around and came forward to the door. He stuck his head over the rail and whinnied to me. He looked me in the eye, and I felt deep down that he didn't want me to leave, that he wanted to tell me something.

After this activity, when we were sharing our experiences with the group, I felt incredibly nervous to share my experience with Reggie. I thought the other participants would reject it as not accurate or possible. I assumed they would judge me and think that I was strange to believe that a horse had something to say to me. This was not the case, however. The participants readily accepted my description and supported my experience, which made my nervousness fall away. I began to relax and become more open to the process. It was clear that I felt a strong connection to Reggie, and he would be the horse that I would work with for the round pen session.

I was anxious and nervous about the round pen session. A fleeting image of running out of the arena and hiding until the sessions were over crossed my mind. I stayed in my chair and watched the participants before me. I had actually thought nothing would happen in my round pen session, that Reggie would completely ignore me and I would look like a fool.

When it was my turn, I walked to the round pen gate. A heavy pain rose in my chest, and fear filled me. Kathy coached me through the Mind Body Method coaching process, which included closing my eyes and allowing my awareness to go inward. During this time, the feeling and thought that kept rising up within me was that I was not a good person. This was something that I had been told in one way or another by everyone in my life since I was a child. I thought I had dealt with that issue long ago, but it resurfaced here again.

Kathy asked me what it was that I wanted from Reggie and what I wanted from the round pen session. I expressed that I really just wanted to connect with Reggie and feel a sense of peace. I didn't need to touch him or pet him; I just wanted to experience that sense of peace. Kathy asked me to open my eyes and take a look at my horse.

To my surprise, Reggie was lying down on the other side of the round pen. He was on his right side with his back toward me. As I entered the pen, I approached Reggie tentatively, fully expecting him to jump up when he heard me approaching. He didn't, though. Instead, he continued to lie there, with me standing at his feet. He began moving his legs, and his eyes rolled into the back of his head in a way that made me feel he was connecting to a place beyond us both, a spiritual place I was unable to see or feel. It is something that is difficult to describe even to this day.

This lasted for a few minutes, until Reggie rolled onto his belly and then stood up. He walked away, to the other side of the pen, leaving me to stand in my same spot, completely speechless. Reggie went to the water bucket and began drinking as if he hadn't had anything to drink for years.

Kathy met me where I was standing to process my experience thus far. As we were processing, I felt overwhelmed with emotion and began crying uncontrollably. Kathy helped me to see that what I was feeling was my false self: "I am not a good person." She helped me to replace my false-self voice with an authentic voice: "I am okay." (I couldn't quite get myself to say that I was a good person.) Kathy coached me several times to speak in my authentic voice, with conviction.

When I finally reached a tone of deep conviction, Reggie turned and came to stand by my side. He placed his barrel parallel with my body. When I reached out and touched him, I felt a flutter in my heart and a sense of peace that I had never expected. Before this, my heart had always been filled with pain. It is difficult to describe the emotions that I was feeling at that moment.

Reggie had placed himself in the most vulnerable of positions. For horses to lie still when someone is standing at their feet is just not natural for them. It goes against the most basic instinct a horse has, self-preservation. Reggie told me in no uncertain terms that I was indeed a good person, someone who could be trusted. Reggie showed me that my negative belief was not authentic but, rather, came from my false self, the self that I needed to let go of.

Reggie then moved away to stand a few feet away from me. I approached him so I could tell him what was in my heart and what I was feeling. I spoke to him and stroked his neck as I released my internal conflict. Reggie remained completely still until I finished speaking to him. When I was done, I thanked him for being with me. He moved away and stood at the pen gate, obviously done with his job.

After the round pen session, I no longer felt anxiety, fear, or the pain in the center of my chest. I felt as though my chest had opened and had filled with warmth and kindness. This was something that I had not expected and had not ever felt at such an intense level. I knew immediately that Reggie had given me a gift of unspeakable proportions. I was genuinely grateful to have been there with him. I was right where I needed to be to experience a powerful healing moment. That night I was very drained emotionally and physically, and I fell into a deep, peaceful sleep.

Since that session with Reggie, I have a new awareness of the false self I carry with me every day. When I start to slide back into my old thought pattern, I think of Reggie and the authentic self he showed me. I no longer think of myself as a bad person and no longer allow anyone else to make me feel that way. I now stand up for myself and my sense of self.

Kathy's Equine Facilitated Learning and coaching program helped me to see how important horses are in my life. After the program I began volunteering at the Medicine Horse Program located in Boulder, Colorado. I started volunteering there in part to be near Reggie and in part to share in the healing that occurs from horses. So much has come from volunteering at the Medicine Horse Program, especially a new sense of accomplishment and confidence. In addition, I have a new direction for my master's degree capstone project, which will now be about the Medicine Horse Program and the effect its program has on at-risk adolescent girls. I know from my own experience with Reggie how horses can elicit profound change, and I want to be a part of that change for someone else. I am thankful every day that I attended the workshop with Kathy that day and met my spirit guide, Reggie.

A note from Kathy:

Reggie's work with Connie exemplifies the profound and unexplainable nature in which horses support the growth of human consciousness. When Connie's session began, Reggie immediately dropped to the ground and became still, something that had never happened in any of my sessions. He was so still that I feared he had simply passed away. I could not see his head, and his barrel did not rise to indicate a breath. A flash of panic moved through me. "Is he okay?" I asked myself.

Finally, Reggie let out a sigh. His breath let me know his body was still on the physical plane, although I was not certain his consciousness was on the same plane. Then Reggie's legs began to twitch and move, just as my dog Suki did when she was in a deep slumber, as if she were dreaming about chasing squirrels.

Reggie seemed far beyond the dream world and was certainly not chasing squirrels. His eyelids began to flutter rapidly, and tremors passed through his whole body. Again I questioned what was happening and felt an urgent sense of responsibility. I thought about stopping the session to check on his well-being: he had not passed fifteen minutes earlier, but I feared he was about to. Then a voice deep within me said, "Wait," so I did.

Deep within Reggie's subconscious, something was moving through his body as he connected to Connie and the emotion she was holding in her body and heart.

That was one of the most profound sessions I have facilitated. Reggie did the most vulnerable thing that a horse can do with a human: he lay down. He had not been half-asleep—instead he completely lost consciousness and moved into another time and place, possibly another layer of consciousness. Connie and Reggie exchanged a secret during their shared moments; it was deep and personal and known only between the two of them.

In their book *Medicine Cards: The Discovery of Power Through the Ways of Animals*, Jamie Dams and David Carson write that the horse represents power. A black horse symbolizes a journey into the Void, where the answers to questions on one's journey can be found. Through moving into the darkness of the Void one can find the light.

Reggie, a black horse with a white diamond on his forehead, may have ventured into the Void and helped to transmute an aspect of Connie's consciousness.

While Reggie lay trembling on the ground, all of Connie's fears and negative feelings toward herself emerged. When she shifted to a more positive view, Reggie rose to his feet to drink water. He turned and walked to her at the precise moment she was engaging her voice of authenticity, one of light.

Horses do things that carry us deep into our subconscious and reveal to us the very part of our being that no longer serves us on our journey. We may feel close to them as we ride on their backs on the earth. However, they also carry us on a spiritual journey, a journey back to our soul.

"In organizations, real power and energy is generated through relationships. The patterns of relationships and the capacities to form them are more important than tasks, functions, roles, and positions."

—Margaret Wheatly, *Leadership and the New Science*

The Call to Leadership

Equine herd dynamics and antics bring richness and learning into corporate and business training programs. Through observing wild and domesticated horse behavior and engaging with horses, participants can quickly see the diverse ways in which horses communicate and bond. Participants come to understand the importance of the initial stages of developing a relationship with a horse and how to translate their learning back to their human relationships.

Horses are social animals that need each other in order to survive. A solitary horse cannot survive alone in the wild without others to share the responsibility for finding food and water or to be on alert for predators so the rest of the herd can sleep. A herd's members have designated tasks. The stallion protects the herd members from predators. The lead mare guides the band to good water and food sources.

Each horse learns where he or she belongs in the band in relationship to all other members. Within the band, each horse also communicates to each other. A stallion firmly puts a young colt in his place when his enthusiasm may propel him into danger. Other times he may take the colt on his patrol of the surrounding areas, mentoring the youngster for his future responsibilities. A mare nurtures her young and eventually teaches them to function on their own.

Communications between herd members are straightforward, direct, and easy to understand. Conflicts are resolved quickly so that the herd can conserve energy. When dangerous or challenging times arise, the herd has the energy to handle the situation. The underlying component ensuring a herd functions well is the ability of its members to relate to each other and to respect the leader. Harmony is necessary for surviving and thriving.

Domestic horses, just like wild horses, find comfort in knowing their place. Put a new horse into an existing herd, and the pecking order shifts and adjusts as the new horse establishes its position. Some will challenge the pecking order in their attempts to become higher in rank.

Public barns often have unstable herds as new members come and go. I once worked at a barn where the horses were moved so often that within months, each began to show signs of being troubled (a clear form of communication), such as anxiety, flightiness, aggression, and/ or depression. In addition, some of them declined in their physical health. Horses need stability in their environments and relationships to feel secure and thrive.

Humans are social animals too, who need to know where they belong in a social or work-related environment, what their function is within the group, and the boundaries for behaviors that create a cohesive community. Without this structure, people struggle in their effort to excel, participate, collaborate, and feel a sense of belonging or safety with the other members.

When a human engages with a horse, a new herd is formed. The horse will first want to know where he or she belongs in the herd in order to feel safe and to survive. The dynamics that play out in this process bring new awareness to the participants. Each horse provides the perfect lesson for each participant. Participants notice that they might shrink back and feel small, allowing the size of the horse to intimidate them. Others discover that they puff up their energy, asserting themselves dramatically and with too much force, unconsciously wanting to feel protected or to create more space for safety. Neither approach is wrong but are simply understood as a refinement of behavior to create a better, more respectful relationship in which leadership comes naturally. The horse often brings to light a behavior to which the participant is blind, one that is hindering his or her performance.

Leadership skills are explored as a participant becomes more active with a horse, asking the horse for forward motion, a change of direction, and for a stop. As the person increases mental focus and intention and develops a core presence—awareness and management of the energy they hold in their physical body—the active work with the horse comes easily. Without it, the client drops back, failing to communicate correctly, sensing their leadership has slipped, because it has.

During a corporate program at the Medicine Horse Program facility in Boulder, participants lined against the fence along the arena to observe herd dynamics. We started with just one horse, Gypsy, a beautiful bay with an air of strength and confidence, a strong presence. I demonstrated the focus of the exercise: Participants would join the herd, establish connection, and then explore leadership by asking for movement.

Boundary sensing involves walking toward the horse, noticing when the animal swishes a tail, sets an eye on you, releases a shiver through his skin, or turns an ear in your direction. These subtle clues are the horse's way of saying, "Hello, I see you, and you are coming into my space." To give the horse respect, the participant notices and acknowledges this communication by pausing momentarily in her step and taking a breath.

Participants entered the arena one at a time. Sometimes the participant practiced increasing her personal presence to create a boundary when a horse moved close into her space. A horse, sensitive to the energy of others, will quickly respond to and, depending on the intention of the person, respect the requested boundary. When the horse does not, it is because the person has begun to feel doubt or fear, and her body subtly shows a loss of core presence.

Others explored what it felt like to ask a horse to move forward and then to stand in the same spot the horse had been standing, just as herd members do—a subtle way of communicating who is going to lead. A phrase I offer in my training programs is, "He who moves his feet the least is leading." A leader directs and guides without expending a lot of energy.

Gypsy, being the lead mare, challenged one person by simply standing her ground. The participant noticed how intimidated he felt by Gypsy's size and presence. When he centered himself in his personal power and confidence and requested her to move, Gypsy slowly moved out of her space, and he walked there to fill it. All the participants took away a visceral experience of the lack of power followed by a sense of centered power. They immediately saw how similar experiences occurred in their working environment with different employees or situations.

After each person explored these exercises with one horse, we changed the herd dynamics by adding two horses, both geldings. Beau, a very tall, beautiful, and lanky Thoroughbred-pinto mix, pushes the boundaries of every person and horse he engages with. Beau loves to play, and for him it is an innocent adolescent game. Beau immediately began to jostle Patrick, the other gelding, while the lead mare, standing a few feet away, observed the interchange without any response. The participants' eyes widened as the horses reared to nip each other's necks and their hooves flew around. We observed their "play" and discussed the dynamics of the herd—how, in a playful way, the two male horses were establishing where they were going to be in this new herd of three. If left alone, they would continue their "play" at intervals, interacting and challenging each other until one solidly established himself as the leader.

Watching a 1,200-pound horse graze in a field or stand in a stall can be a very calming and grounding experience. Watching two 1,200-pound horses jostling, rearing, and twisting their necks around each other is entirely different. This interaction can evoke fear and trepidation in humans, as it should. To engage with such animals without any experience or knowledge about horses would be dangerous. When watching this sort of demonstration, fear is a *healthy* instinctive response. Unfortunately, our culture promotes and rewards behaviors that override natural fear responses in order to reach the goal. It was revealing to see what several of the participants chose to do with their fear during the next sessions.

After Beau and Patrick slowed down their antics, the horse handler removed one, which left Beau with Gypsy. We watched a more gentle exchange of energy between them. Her position already established from previous interactions, she dismissed Beau with a few head swings, and he listened. I invited participants to come into the arena with me to experience working with two horses. Immediately, one woman volunteered. I coached her as she began to set a boundary with Beau and then ask him to move away from her. Gypsy then came toward her, and she also moved her away. The woman was positive, enthusiastic, and remained grounded in her body, and the horses responded accordingly.

Phil, another participant, was very tuned in and sensitive to others and their emotions but had no training or skills for how to manage his high sensitivities. He mentioned to me that often he felt so much it was confusing for him. He had experienced a strong response to the geldings' demonstration of jostling. I replaced Beau with the less dynamic gelding, Patrick, to decrease the intensity.

Phil and I walked into the arena and talked privately about the importance of being congruent with what he was feeling and thinking. I coached him using the Mind Body Method. Phil struggled to find the words to express what he was feeling in his core presence. In addition, his fears provoked him to blurt out questions such as: "What if they don't listen to me?" "Can they hurt me?" and "Will that horse rear up while I am in here?" After I answered his questions and addressed his worries, he set his intention to first connect with and then ask for movement with one of the horses.

Phil approached Gypsy, and she began to move forward. Then she stopped and looked at him, testing his leadership and conviction, and then looked away toward the open pasture, not at all interested in joining up. Phil seemed distant and lacked clear communication. His hands showed a slight twitch, his breath was a bit shallow, and he kept his eyes on Gypsy. He avoided my questions about his emotional state and the thoughts he was holding. He kept trying to hide his true feelings. He had, in fact, hesitated to come into the arena with the horses even after Patrick replaced Beau. I knew I could not push him into being "real" and in the moment and that his defensive posturing at this time was what he needed for protection.

He continued to approach each horse with trepidation and eventually became frustrated because he was not getting the results he wanted. Patrick would move for him, but not with any enthusiasm or respect. Gypsy would simply glance at him, then turn her head and stare straight ahead, standing her ground, not giving him much attention at all. I coached him to see how his thoughts of worry and doubt would send each of the horses away from him; when he spoke from an honest place, each would begin to look at him with curiosity.

Phil began to see, first-hand, how he could keep the horses' attention, simply by acknowledging, to himself, what he was feeling and thinking. Phil shared that he is so sensitive to others' emotions that he often becomes overwhelmed, and he struggles to lead others. What Phil was unable to achieve within himself (congruency), what he most wanted to avoid (fear), was communicated silently to the horse; for the horse this was a more powerful form of communication than his words or actions. The horse responded to what Phil was attempting to ignore. Phil observed how these very same patterns or interactions showed up in his leadership with his human partners. He understood that to be a better leader, he needed, first and foremost, to have an honest relationship with himself. If he could not be honest with himself, then how could he expect anyone else to trust his advice or input?

Melissa, who next came into the arena, began to have a similar experience. The horses moved a bit for her, but they did not respond to her with respect or enthusiasm. Her body was stiff, and her breath became shallow. We stood at the far end of the arena as I began to coach her through the Mind Body Method just as I had with Phil. Gypsy moved to the opposite side of the arena, the farthest point away from us, where she nibbled on some small blades of grass along the fence

Melissa looked at me with open, wide, and willing eyes as we began the coaching conversation. She first admitted that she felt a strong sensation in her solar plexus area. No sooner had she said this than Gypsy lifted her head and stared directly at her. Melissa kept her eyes on Gypsy as she began to identify the feeling she was holding in her solar plexus. She said she felt anxious and fearful. I asked her what she feared the most. She said that she was afraid that Gypsy would reject her and not want to join up. She did not want to fail in front of her colleagues. A tear dropped out of her eye and she let out a deep breath, the relief at getting the truth out naturally relaxing her.

Gypsy, not missing a beat, turned her whole body and walked softly and directly across the arena right to Melissa's side. The mare paused and then took one step closer to Melissa. She then placed her nose on Melissa's solar plexus. Gypsy exhaled a breath and then moved her nose to Melissa's heart and exhaled again. Melissa began to bat her eyelashes in a feeble attempt to hold back the surge of emotion that was passing through her body. A smile spread across her mouth, and she let out a deep sigh.

Because Melissa had dared to be real, to tell the truth, the horse sensed the tension disappearing and joined up with her. Gypsy had not offered this with any of the men, as each had retained mixed messages in the emotional tension in their bodies.

When Melissa began to work with Gypsy by asking for movement around the arena, Gypsy complied without resistance. Melissa began to build a relationship with Gypsy, not through force, dominance, control, or manipulation, but through being heart-centered and vulnerable and getting honest with herself about her fears. Once Melissa had removed her own resistance to her internal feeling by acknowledging the emotion and the message, she was able regain her ground and power.

Both Phil and Melissa experienced first-hand that their emotional states affected their abilities to be a leader. Creating internal integrity by listening to and honoring emotion as information enables the flow of leadership, as Melissa experienced. Controlling one's emotional reactions and responses while simultaneously understanding their purpose and how to respond to them dramatically increases one's ability to be an *authentic* leader. It is about listening to the messages contained by the body wisdom and not stepping over them, as Phil attempted to do. It is about the power of processing those feelings and emotions through the filters of the heart versus the head.

A message from the body can be as simple as a gut feeling that lets you know a person is being dishonest, whether the timing is not right or is absolutely right, or when a partnership will not serve you. Often in environments where one's head is busy being productive, these key messages are lost or dismissed as invalid or paranoid. The messages clarify direction so that valuable time is saved, and one can more effectively lead and collaborate with others.

People are very much like horses in that they have the ability to sense the intuitive, instinctive form of communication that is invisible to the eye. People can naturally sense when something is just not right or slightly off with another individual. They may not always listen to the message they are receiving, and they may not be able to put a finger on exactly what it is, but they will sense unconsciously and often respond in an unconscious manner to the unacknowledged condition. Phil experienced this sensation and learned he must improve his ability to listen to his feelings and intuition and to distinguish the messages they hold. He connected the similarities between how the horse responded to him and how his employees often respond to him; when he was emotionally incongruent, there was distance and distrust.

People (and horses) can tune into any incongruence within a leader and the intentions they hold behind their words and actions. Who you are as a leader is just as important as what you do. The authentic leader realizes this and actively seeks higher levels of congruence, or inner integrity, and emotional intelligence to improve his leadership skills and to achieve higher levels of success.

Many professional development programs suggest that there is a leader within every person. I take exception to this opinion. I agree that every mentally and emotionally healthy individual has the power to self-regulate his or her thoughts, emotions, and actions as the leader of one's own life and destiny. However, I feel that only a few individuals have the *natural* capacity and *drive* to lead and influence others to greater heights of awareness, change, and movement. In the wild, not every bachelor stallion has his own band. It may be that he does not possess the chemistry or drive to be a herd stallion.

Not every person is a *natural* leader, nor do they necessarily desire to be. In the fourteen years that my work has been focused on helping individuals grow and become more conscious, I have observed many obstacles that people encounter as they attempt to step into a life based in purpose and passion, toward their right livelihood and authentic expression. People fear physically breaking away from their already established community, of losing the existing band that they belong to.

Many people lack the ability to become a leader because they lack the capacity or the strength and willingness to take a risk. Every step to wholeness and higher levels of authenticity involves risk. Will my friends and family grow with me? Will my employer still want me in the company if I speak up? Will I fail? Will I succeed?

Not every person will rise to great heights of leadership, nor do they want to. If we all became leaders, then who would follow? How would things get accomplished? If everyone wanted to be a leader, then everyone would bicker and squabble about what to do, how to do it, and who needs to do what, continually failing to arrive at agreements. The person who wishes to follow is a valid, much needed, and honorable part of the whole. Not because such people lack the ability to face their fears and venture into new territory and become blind followers, but because they authentically offer their gift to the world or society by their position.

The bachelor horse in the wild must not only experience displacement from his original herd; he then has to risk the loss of the new herd, and possibly his life, when he challenges a stallion in order to obtain a mare. He risks everything. Humans take risks, too, every time they seek to grow and evolve. How we approach that risk determines how we live. Can we venture out, aware of the risk, and still move toward our vision with confidence? Or do we shrink back and keep ourselves safe in the existing herd, even though we intrinsically know our higher calling is to step out and shine like a stallion? Humans determine if they are hiding in fear, living in harmony, or venturing into worlds unknown by listening to each one's calling and knowing from the heart.

There are several questions I ask myself as I feel the urge, or hear the *call,* to lead:

- Do I find deep inner harmony in my current position? Is it fulfilling?

- At the end of my life, will I feel satisfied with who I am and what I have accomplished?

- What compels me to move forward?

- What is the purpose in my desire to lead? How does it, and who does it, serve?

- Do I know myself well enough to lead others?

The questions I ask myself, and offer others, as I explore *authentic leadership* are:

- Am I being conscious of how my thoughts, feelings, and actions shape my world and affect others?

- Am I leading from my truth and my heart?

- Do I seek harmony and cohesiveness in relationships first and goals second?

- Do I inspire others to their potential and truth?

- If I choose to fight, how and why is it worth my vital life force energy?

Whether you are washing dishes, raising children, saving animals, building skyscrapers, or donating millions to nonprofit organizations, what and how you contribute through self-leadership and your core being is your journey and your responsibility. How you affect others will determine the quality of your leadership.

Not everyone is born to lead others, but we all have the potential to become leaders of the self. A leader must listen to her spiritual connections, emotional information, physical instincts, and intellect. Her energy must extend beyond herself with the desire to touch lives, make a difference, and achieve visions through being in grace. She must believe in the grace of authentic power and her ability to express it. Listen deeply to your whole being, like a horse, and you will hear more: more about a passion, a purpose, and something you know you must pursue. Your purpose calls you forth because living without it would not be living. What is your call to leadership?

"Far back, far back in our dark soul the horse prances . . . The horse, the horse! The symbol of surging potency and power of movement, of action . . ."

—D. H. Lawrence

The Rebel

My path with mustangs began in May of 2007, when I adopted a six-year-old Pryor Mountain mustang from Ginger Kathrens.

Ginger is the Emmy award–winning filmmaker of the PBS documentary *Cloud: Wild Stallion of the Rockies*, which captures the essence of the Pryor Mountain wild horses and documents their herd dynamics and lifestyle. Her nonprofit organization, The Cloud Foundation, is dedicated to the preservation of historically significant and genetically unique wild horses on public lands, including Cloud's herd in Montana.

The DNA of the Pryor Mountain mustangs has been traced back to the horses brought into North America by the Spanish conquistadors. Ginger has filmed one stallion, whom she has named Cloud, throughout his life. Cloud possesses a fierce independence, charisma, and the drive for his own family band. Watching Ginger's films inspired me to explore how the wild horses can teach humans about leadership, community, and communication.

During a conversation with Ginger, she mentioned five mustangs that had been deemed untrainable and unadoptable by the Bureau of Land Management (BLM). She had removed the mustangs from a BLM holding facility and placed them in a training program at a Colorado prison. The mustangs were subsequently available for adoption in the spring of 2007. I heard myself say, "I will take one."

I jumped from working with a well-trained and well-behaved Quarter Horse to a little 14.2-hand mustang that had survived in the wild all of his life. This little horse with a fierce spirit and a big heart I named Corazon de la Montana, or Heart of the Mountain. He was later nicknamed Romeo for his amorous behavior toward any mare he could find. Corazon's color is officially called brown, but he is essentially black, with just a little bit of brown around his nose.

During the first eight months of our relationship, I worked with Corazon to gain his trust and to understand his nature. Some days were filled with delight and wonder over his keen intelligence, while other days were filled with frustration and sometimes tears as I struggled to find common ground.

Life often presents us with unpredictable moments, challenging us to expand our capacity to relate. It is not always easy or joyful, but the opportunity is there. Corazon consistently offers me these opportunities.

After months of training, I reached limitations in my abilities. I needed help in teaching Corazon to accept a saddle and a rider, so I enrolled him in a program with a local trainer. Hugh, the trainer, eventually brought Corazon around to accept a saddle. In order to work with Hugh, Corazon had been moved from his herd at one ranch to a new ranch environment to live in a solitary paddock, with only one neighbor horse across the fence to connect with.

Hugh was sick over the Christmas holidays, and I was unable to go to the ranch. Without my knowing it, Corazon was handled very little for a week. When I finally arrived, he came to the gate immediately. I noticed that his playmate in the next paddock was no longer there. I haltered Corazon and took him out of the paddock for a stroll down the driveway.

Corazon and I often walk together, and it is always very enjoyable. Corazon whinnied several times as we left the paddock area. The muscles in his neck were tight with alertness and his stride energetic. He seemed to have grown two feet in height. His energy was palpable.

We walked down the long driveway. The wind began to blow, and the thirty horses in a large open field raced around. Corazon's nose darted out to challenge me. He shook and threw his head, tugging on the lead line, threatening my leadership by wanting to get away. He stomped his foot with frustration. His eyes watched my every move, his dissatisfaction more than clear.

My hand clenched the rope and my boots skittered on the ice-packed drive as I searched for stable footing. My stomach turned, and my nerves got on edge. A bitter wind hit my face, filled my ears with stinging hailstones. I began to question my sanity, but I was dedicated to reconnecting with my horse.

I was invisible to Corazon. My nerves began to become unglued, and I felt stretched in my ability to manage him. He had not acted this way since the very first week that he had arrived in my care.

Corazon stared at the herd of thirty horses eating hay in the snow-covered field. More whinnies pierced my ears and reached the others in the herd. The replying whinnies did not help to calm my horse. Corazon wanted to jerk away from me and run to what he knew: to be within a larger herd, working as a group to survive the cold winter days and nights.

I turned him around and headed to the indoor arena. His head only became more active, pulling back to the others. Every few yards he planted his feet, refusing to move forward. Each time I positioned myself in a safe spot and gently pulled his lead line until there was tension. Whenever he did not give to the line, my other hand twirled the free end of the lead rope near his backside to motivate him to move forward. I stopped the twirling, releasing pressure, as soon as his feet moved.

The indoor arena was crispy cold, but at least the wind could not reach us. At its far side was a small round pen, about forty feet in width instead of the standard sixty feet. My intention was for us to come back into relationship, to get Corazon's mind with me and for his energy to come down several notches. Inside the pen Corazon continued to throw his head and stomp his front hoof. I remained standing in the center, unwilling to move or to let his tantrum affect me.

I then removed his halter and began to work with him at liberty. He had nothing holding him back, and I had only my body language as a means of communication. He immediately faced away from me, pointed his butt to me, and began a kicking festival. His hooves sprayed gravel onto my coat and in my face. He then began to run around, stomping with excessive energy, his head shaking back and forth. My little horse had returned to his wild, expressive nature.

Suddenly my heart was racing and my breath was short and trapped high in my throat. I focused on my breath as I do when achieving a difficult yoga pose, counting to six during both the inhalation and exhalation. My inner landscape was hardly calm and composed, and my body was shaking. I needed to control my own internal arousal state as he challenged my leadership. I kept breathing and focusing, acknowledging my inner experience but not allowing it to rise up into frustration or anger or to send me running out of the round pen filled with fear. I began to repeat a mantra in my mind, "This will pass. Stay calm."

I remained in the center and directed Corazon around the pen. He crashed around and around the pen at top speed but got nowhere. He threw his butt toward me to show his displeasure. Holding my ground in the center, I twirled my rope at his hindquarters, sending him in the direction I wanted him to move instead of the direction that he wanted.

He continued his kicking and bucking. I did not move, but I kept him away from me by requesting through my thoughts and body language that he move around the outer circle. It was not my intention to tire him out: I wanted instead for him to release excessive energy. Each time he moved around the perimeter, my breath began to sink deeper into my body. The internal shaking became a rattle, then a slight tremble, and eventually dissolved. The mantra continued to flow through my mind. I began to work with his body, asking him to move back and forth. I did not make him work extra hard or break into a big sweat, but I did work with him until I felt he was paying attention.

Nine months earlier when Corazon came into my life, he had done the very same thing. He threw a fit, angry that he was not free to run with the other horses and that he was in a confined area. He would run from me when I tried to halter him and eventually reared and bucked at my attempts. At that time I left the round pen, scared out of my wits, believing that he wanted to kill me or at least stomp me into the ground. This time, understanding his perspective and nature better, I saw that he was not out to intentionally hurt me. He was, however, giving some very direct communications.

Continuing my work with him in the round pen, I offered Corazon moments to experience release from movement and to come toward me without frustration. Eventually Corazon did come to me. We stood together, and as I scratched his withers, he exhaled and began to lick and chew. I exhaled too. Both of us were beginning to relax, and he was reconnecting with me. After a bit more movement and work together, he completely relaxed in his body and mind. It was a good time to stop, so we walked back to his paddock.

I left the ranch doubting my ability to work with Corazon. His ingrained wildness concerned me, and I wondered whether it would ever completely diminish. I found myself thinking about everything that I had possibly done wrong that day. I took full responsibility for his behavior. I judged his behavior as wrong and inappropriate. Soon my thoughts and then my spirits began to tumble into negativity: My horse was clearly unhappy; I had made the wrong decision to bring him to the new ranch; and I had no right to be working with him. He was beyond my skill level.

After talking with like-minded horse person and fellow equine-learning facilitator Karen, I came back into my mental and emotional center. Karen pointed out to me that Corazon had not shown his best behavior; in fact, he had been rather aggressive and bratty. He had acted like an adolescent because he was an adolescent. She reminded me that he was only six and a half years old and had only been in the human world for about one year.

Karen pointed out the progress in our relationship. She noted that my response to his behavior had changed. She helped me see everything that was right about the situation and helped me to shift to a positive perspective. Instead of running away, as I had in May, I had stood my ground in the center of the round pen. Instead of choosing to be angry or fearful, I remained centered and calm. My ability to be with him in all of his various emotional states was shifting. She pointed out to me how my emotional agility had developed, now allowing me to be in stressful, emotionally charged situations without reacting in a negative manner toward him. I did not let him run over me, nor did I lash out at him. If I had lashed out at him, we would have gone to war, and I would have lost. I simply kept working with him until his energy came back down and he adjusted his rebellious attitude.

I also realized that doubting myself was a waste of time. My next step of progress would be to release negative thoughts. Corazon was not too wild or aggressive, even though a few people at the ranch implied so.

Corazon and I are well bonded; I know what his needs are. He needs to be with other horses, and his needs were not being met. When I first arrived at the ranch I had asked Hugh to make sure my horse was either with other horses or at least had a friend over the fence. I later found out Hugh had moved his paddock neighbor, and Corazon had been completely alone for about four days. It was not intentional, just simply what was needed on the ranch. The ranch also was not ready to put him out with the other geldings because another mustang had demonstrated very aggressive behavior the previous year (mustangs on that ranch carried an unfortunate label based on breed, versus the philosophy that each individual horse has its own character).

As I chatted with Karen, I realized where my mind goes after a day of being challenged by Corazon. Typically I make myself believe that what had happened was wrong. I judge either Corazon or myself, thinking that things *should* be different. Acceptance means that things *are* exactly as they should be. A relationship with Corazon means that I deal with the emotions and the behaviors that he moves through as he adjusts to the human world. Nothing needs to change. I must remain patient, strong, and peaceful in my requests. Otherwise respect diminishes between the two of us.

I learned to trust my inner guidance, intuition, and gut feelings in regard to Corazon's needs and training. He counts on me to be his spokesperson. If I am not, he will let me know in his way. There will be times that I may be wrong about what he needs. However, to doubt myself also means that I do not respect my own wisdom and that I have let weakness creep into my consciousness. It is my responsibility to remain positive in my mind about our relationship.

What is respect? We earn respect. Respect is not implied or bestowed because of one's position or authority. I cannot assume that Corazon will respect me simply because he is my responsibility in a human-oriented environment. Respect reflects strength and power that is based in caring, curiosity, and consistency. Each time I stand my ground with Corazon and remain firm and unwavering without lashing out or being mean, I gain his trust, which only leads to more respect. I must not assume "bad behavior" or put his reponses into that box. Instead, I must understand that behavior and body language are the primary ways he can communicate with me. It is my responsibility to seek to understand what he communicates through his behavior and which of his needs are not being filled.

Lastly, I must remember that we have much to learn on this path of growth and that the process will take time. There will be frustrating moments when I feel no connection or when Corazon becomes rebellious to my requests. It is my job as leader to rise to the challenge that is presented and stay consistent in my nature, my communication, and my approach with him. Each time he pushes me to my limits (patience, boundaries, communication), he gives me the gift of an opportunity to be a better leader and person.

It is also my responsibility to remain safe at all times. I held my ground with Corazon this time because instinctively it felt like the right thing to do. I am not suggesting that others respond to their horses the same way in highly energetically charged situations. Each situation is different and requires different responses. As a leader you must know your limits.

How often do we approach challenging situations in life as opportunities for growth? What is our response to situations that take us to the edge of our composure? Do we lash out, becoming an aggressor, or pull back and become a victim?

Corazon teaches me every day the versatility required to relate to another being. The intensity and pure honesty of his expression takes me to new levels of energetic and emotional arousal and forces me to stretch my ability to be patient. He teaches me that to know him means to listen to him and understand him. I must be curious and ask what he is communicating, as his needs may be more pronounced than a domesticated horse. Through this process of searching to understand, I have gained more patience in my human relationships.

I believe we must rise to the challenges in our relationships. We must not punish or shame, dismiss or desert others for behaviors that make us feel uncomfortable. Our job is to stretch our hearts and minds to what is possible and "right" in every situation. We must find the silver lining of understanding. As we do so, our ability to plumb the most difficult situations creates trust, intimacy, and respect for our self and for others.

"Love the animals, love the plants, love everything. If you love everything, you will perceive the divine mystery in things. Once you perceive it, you will begin to comprehend it better every day. And you will come at last to love the whole world with an all-embracing love."

—Fyodor Dostoyevsky

Like a Horse

After several years of working with people and horses, I have formulated the key foundational components of my Equine Facilitated Learning and coaching programs. Individuals moving through life transitions and seeking new awareness about their passion and purpose seek me out for sessions to learn about themselves through the wisdom of the horse. Other individuals come seeking help in healing past trauma and fears or to move to greater levels of functioning and achievement. Corporate groups implement my leadership and emotional intelligence programs for their executives and managers. Individuals of all ages benefit from equine-based learning programs; I am privileged to work with children from age six and up and with adults into their late sixties. There seems to be no limit to what is possible when it comes to employing horses as teachers: the field is new, it is creative. It has inspired many talented, imaginative individuals and many horses, who are not only willing and seem to enjoy the work but also thrive in serving this way.

As you have seen in previous chapters, learning sessions can range from facilitating riders on horseback to assisting riders and nonriders on the ground, with the horse next to them. Horses offer humans several gifts of growth and discovery. The gifts come from the horse, by the horse simply being a horse. Horses offer their natural state of being to enrich human awareness of self and others. Through interacting with a horse, the human learns to respect the differences between individuals (horse or human). In learning horses' social traits, we become more aware of our impression upon them. Horses consistently reflect the essence, intention, emotion, and energy of the person interacting with them, even if the human is not willing, able, and open enough to consider it. The human who engages with and seeks the gift of a horse as a mirror for self and accepts the responsibility to be an eternal student in all relationships benefits in many ways, including increases in personal power, trust of the flow of life, creative expression, heart opening, and the ability to assert and speak one's truth. An added bonus is the ability to tune in and intuit on levels previously not experienced. Often clients are blessed with the most profound experience, an ability to encounter the divine mystery on a cellular level, discovering the interconnection of all beings on the planet, regardless of species.

Power Arises from Physical Presence

What horses do best is graze. Grazing is a relaxed state of being, fully integrated into the environment, and fully present in the moment. The sole purpose of grazing is to eat and nurture the body. My equine-based programs do not implement big agendas or to-do lists. Each has its own intention or focus, and all learning is achieved through observing, sharing, being present, and exploring relationships with horses. The key teachings occur when engaging with the horse in several different activities that include: relationship-building skills, active work that focuses on movement, leadership practices on the ground, integrative awareness while riding, and intuitive approaches for horsemanship.

The equine-based learning and coaching programs I offer essentially teach people, while interacting with horses, to be more "like a horse" in their nature, to explore the power of being present, to "graze" in their senses, to gather impressions, and to reflect on the experience. To be more like a horse, one must have an awareness of one's physical body, sensations, gut feelings—the subtle clues one receives through the senses about others in the environment, or the environment itself. Being like a horse also includes being aware of one's emotions, energy, and body language and of those belonging to others around oneself; knowing how to co-operate in community; and understanding the importance of being a leader or a follower. Participants learn to understand herd dynamics and that this social structure differs very little from human social structures. To be horse-like means that one has the versatility to lead, follow, assert, receive, sense, communicate, and collaborate through partnership. It also implies a particular alignment to one's self and owning one's authentic expression.

When I speak of being like a horse, I mean horses in a relaxed state, when they are fully grounded and coherent in their environment. They are focusing on the internal messages of the body and guts with the outer environment. Hypersensitive, flighty, and unstable horses would not fall into this category. Because of their extra-sensitive natures, however, these horses are some of the best teachers. They quickly respond to individuals who are not body-centered. When these horses experience humans tuning more deeply into their body awareness through the Mind Body Method coaching process, they also more than likely become more grounded and stable in their environment. Alexandra Lowen, M.D., in his book *Bioenergetics*, states:

> *A healthy person can alternate these two points of focus easily and rapidly so that almost at the same time one is aware of one's bodily self and of the environment. Such a person is mindful of what is happening to himself, as well as what is happening to others. But not everyone has this ability. Some people become too mindful of themselves and develop an embarrassing self-consciousness. Others are so mindful of what is going on around them that they lose consciousness of the self. This is frequently true of hypersensitive individuals.*

Through the process of learning about horses, my clients become more emotionally, mentally, and physically integrated, able to access all of their resources (internal and external) at any given time to direct and lead and maintain their grounding. The horses directly mirror individuals who have stepped away from authentic feeling and thinking processes. The horse offers an instant, live, thousand-pound biofeedback mechanism for learning.

Our world is growing more and more fast-paced and information-based than ever before. We are developing our technology to realms unimaginable even twenty-five years ago. The momentum continues to build; almost every mechanically operated tool, appliance, and machine we use now has or will soon have computerized components. Everything is becoming programmed.

Fourteen years ago when I became a massage therapist (and then a Life Coach shortly after that), I experienced the benefits of slowing down my life, reconnecting to the wisdom of my body, and being present in my life. The more present I became, the more the choices I made in my life were based on my core values. At the time, I knew I wanted others to experience the process of coming back into their bodies and to develop the ability to not only be present but have presence, and to do all of this while being in nature. It had all seemed rather farfetched to me. I questioned who would really need that and who would hire me to help them with it. Now, many years later, I am seeing the stresses of the average person's life and the need for such a service. My client load and the results of the work I am doing with individuals confirm that, yes, slowing down and getting present have many great benefits, and people need this and want it, even if it is only for a few hours or days. What they learn in that time transfers back into their everyday lives, helping them to make important decisions based on a deeper level of heart-based, body-centered wisdom.

To live a life based in purpose and service requires self-awareness. It requires people to be intentional about where they are putting their focus and energy on a day-to-day basis. It requires people to shift their intention and actions into the communities, jobs, and events that most reflect their key values, not what society or their families may be telling them to value and do. All good life decisions are based in a response to one's life, rather than in reaction to external circumstances, which often convey a false sense of urgency. It is impossible to respond except with a quiet mind and a centered body. Most people are living reaction-based lives that lack centering and grounding in the body. They spin from their heads and try to catch up with over-committed lifestyles.

A common theme in both my life-coaching work and in the work I do with humans and horses together is that when clients are willing to utilize the tools I offer to help them become more centered in their physical body, the horses respond positively, relaxing with them and holding a space of deep peace. Coming back into the physical body can be a daunting task for many, especially those who may have become very bound to their heads due to lifestyle patterns, old trauma, or simply being unconscious. With the support of the horse, by implementing the processes and the tools, humans I coach often reach greater levels of discovery and awareness than they could have reached on their own.

My horse Moon often demonstrates his natural ability to anchor and help my clients go more deeply into their physical bodies. Moon is a large horse, and his energy is soft and expansive, yet very solid and strong. At his former home, his job was to be a ranch horse. Moon has an uncanny ability to focus in on an object (cow or human) and hold his whole awareness on that object for great lengths of time. He remains fully aware of what is around him but offers his full attention and presence to the object on which he is focusing. In doing so during client sessions, Moon creates a space that is grounded and safe for the client to experience. It may be similar to the atmosphere you feel when you walk into a counselor or massage therapist's office, or what you feel when you have a conversation with someone that you feel comfortable enough to confide in and allow your emotions to come forth, confident that the person hears you. It is a sacred space shared between two individuals. Sometimes a person can experience this response by simply being in the presence of a great teacher, healer, or shaman. The presence of that person evokes an instant reduction of stress, a relaxation, perhaps a sudden flow of tears, allowing for a different, more authentic experience to transpire. People and animals who naturally create a sacred space that we find comfort in offer us the time and place to let down our protective guard. It is an unquantifiable feeling—nothing solid to measure; simply a feeling—a feeling of being touched by grace. Moon, like many horses, creates this space.

After working with Moon, many of my clients report that they feel more contained within and aware of their physical bodies. They connect more easily to the sensations in their stomach, throat, shoulders, lower back, and hips. Some say the pain they were carrying has subsided. During one session, Moon simultaneously stretched his neck high, his back legs out, and his front legs forward with a client who was doing the same thing, stretching her back, her legs, her arms, and neck. It was as if he were leading a morning yoga class, helping this client come back into her physical body. After completing her stretches with him, she noted that the back pain she felt when she had arrived was gone, apparently released through her session with Moon.

The polo ponies taught me a lot about being sensitive to the boundaries of herd members. I practiced asserting my boundary with them and then I moved, asking them to move out of their space, and then I stood in the space where they had stood. At that time in my life Junta had much greater power in my relationship with her than I had. I diminished in her presence. Now, since applying my Mind Body Method principles with the horses, they have taught me how to become more integrated and aware. My guess is that now I would have no problem owning my space and asking Junta to move out of her space. My level of personal power has increased dramatically now that I am more body-centered and free of the former trauma from being thrown and dragged. My intention is always to ask the horse for movement with respect, through clear communication and intention, with a sense of equal partnership, not dominance and aggression. I was capable then of dominating with a whip or stick if I really wanted to, or if I felt truly threatened. That approach was valid in that I was self-protecting. The goal today, or what I seek, is to understand at higher levels, thus removing the fear.

Some horses may test humans' boundaries. They constantly come into the client's space, nudging relentlessly, subtly maneuvering the person leading them, shifting the direction of the duo and taking leadership. These antics mirror a weakness in the client, an area of growth ready to shift and expand into new possibilities. Taking the opportunity for growth, the client learns how to be clear in their thoughts and intentions about their boundaries and how to establish those boundaries with the horse. To learn how to ask and obtain a boundary, one must engage the *whole being* to securely establish it and gain respect from the horse.

It can be a powerful experience for any person who struggles with articulating and achieving good boundaries in their life to work with horses. When they learn how to set a boundary with a 1,200-pound horse, it becomes a lot easier to set boundaries with a rambunctious eight-year-old, an aggressive co-worker, or the teenage friend who is pushing for sex or involvement with drugs. "Just say 'No'" becomes second nature after you say "No" to twelve hundred pounds of massive muscle.

The bottom line is that successful boundary setting is not achieved solely through our thinking head. Instead, the whole being must be engaged. The request comes from the power center of the body, the gut level. Spoken with conviction, the request comes from deep within, not the surface. Starting in the lower belly, the request moves through the whole body with intention and commitment. This happens when the person requesting that boundary believes they have the right to it, with both horses and with humans.

If you are thinking that you already have boundaries down and that a horse can't teach you much about them, you may be fooling yourself. The more I coach people of all ages and all levels of consciousness and awareness, the more I find that boundaries continue to be a part of one's evolution and growth. As any person grows and refines and redefines who they are, he or she learns to focus and channel energy toward an authentic expression or life purpose. This act requires that the internal resources not only identify new boundaries to establish at every level of growth but new, subtler ways to establish them. Boundaries are not brick walls; rather, they are like a fence dividing a pasture. They define a space and still allow wind, light, rain, leaves, and smaller animals to pass through the space. Having a good sense of your own boundaries and personal space is a way of walking in the world with so much respect and honor for one's self and others that it never feels like a defined boundary, but rather a dance of the self interacting with others and the world.

The ability to be present and body-centered is the first key foundational component of learning with the horses. Regardless if it is standing your ground, establishing a boundary, sensing your inner physical landscape, or being tuned into the outer environment, it all happens from within, from the inside of your being to the outside reality. If you want to fully experience life, there is one way to do it: sense your own inner landscape, in relationship to the outer, take it all in, respond, and allow it to pass through. The easier it happens, the more horse-like you are.

Emotion and Energy, the Language of Equus

The second key foundational component of learning with horses in equine-based experiences is how horses teach humans to be emotionally agile and energetically aware.

Horses respond to changes in the climate; the winds that rise when a storm is about to blow in bring with them smells from a far distance. Horses respond to other horses in trouble within their own herd or in the distance. They whinny when a horse is loaded into a trailer and taken off the property and whinny when the trailer returns. They are sensitive to the energy of their environment and to the energy of each of their herd members. When my clients come to work with horses, I remind them that they are becoming part of the herd. They must learn to understand the nature of horses to better relate to them and create a connection with them. Through the Mind Body Method process, I coach them to become fully aware of the emotional energy they are carrying simultaneously with their thoughts. Through that process a part of them that they were ignoring comes to the surface, releasing the energy and vibration of that emotion. Their emotional well-being becomes strengthened and whole, integrated and congruent.

The horse, in turn, consistently expresses his or her appreciation through relaxing; one leg drops and a hip becomes cocked, the head lowers, licking and chewing begin, and the eyelids soften. The client is now becoming aware of what their emotional body is expressing and listens to that energy for their advancement, instead of ignoring it or projecting it out onto the horse. Amigo (Chapter Four) helped me learn this. I focused on staying grounded in my body and on being honest with myself, and with him, about what I was feeling. I did not ignore my fear, but instead I acknowledged and gained power through it without having to run away or dissociate.

When experiencing an emotionally congruent client, the horse returns to a relaxed state. Amigo, when working with me, dropped his head and began to lick and chew once I was fully emotionally congruent and honest with him. Flash demonstrated her willingness to stand with those who were congruent about their experience of grief, but she ran away from a woman who was struggling to be fully present and aware of her emotional state of being. From a mutually understood state and being aware and congruent emotionally, a person can achieve a partnership with the horse that brings greater levels of success and understanding. The relationship is based on the respect for the horse's sensitivity to the intentions, attitudes, and emotional energy of others and to the timing of approach and retreat and the energetic boundaries present. The mysterious connection between beings that many seek is present and alive.

For every frustrated horse handler you see trying to load a horse into a trailer, likely there is a frustrated horse also trying to be loaded. Emotion, which is very contagious around horses, often amplifies without the awareness of the human involved. Simply noticing emotions that are rising and then returning to center and taking responsibility for one's emotional reactions or responses helps settle the horse. Most people try to settle the horse when they are going into fear in their predatory body, when their body releases the fight or flight hormones. It is very difficult for the other herd member, the horse, to calm down, when its handler is in this state. The handler has lost his or her power to lead.

The same applies to circumstances of life. A leader who has become unconscious of emotional energy, whether it is rising from the self or activated by those close by through contagion, loses the ability to lead with clear power. The situation is tainted by the unconscious energy of the emotion, affecting all decisions and manners of interaction. When we acknowledge the energy's presence and accept it, we are expressing it whether we intend to or not, and congruency results.

Individuals in workshops sometimes experience fear, performance anxiety, frustration, or other emotions as they begin their work with the horse. Numerous times I have watched the horses reflect or mirror back these emotional states back to the client. The horse's energy becomes amplified. The animal might start to pace anxiously along the fence line. She might start to paw the ground with impatience and frustration, or she might start to whinny to call for her nearby herd mates who are more grounded and calm. She needs their steady, strong presence to feel safe. Each and every time I coach clients to honestly articulate what they are feeling and express the thoughts that are accompanying those feelings, the horse's energy begins to decrease. The substance of a client's thoughts or feelings (positive or negative) matters less than whether he or she communicates them honestly.

When a horse has experienced trauma from a human who simultaneously projected a negative emotion such as anger, rage, or hate, often the presence of the emotional energy alone can send the horse back into a similar response to the one it had during the traumatic event.

Horses read emotions as energy and communication. For them, the feeling each member has in the herd travels through the herd like sound waves. Think of a time when you listened to musicians perform at a virtuoso level. Often their notes bring an emotional response to the body such as sadness, aliveness, tension, or a complete joyful moment. Emotions travel in much the same manner as musical notes or other sound waves.

The difference between horses and humans is that humans become hung up about feeling their emotions or allowing others to observe any sort of emotion. The human's ego, the fear of being vulnerable, shuts down one of the most powerful assets a person has: the ability to feel one's emotions rising, to understand why they are rising, and to be fully present and centered in the experience. Such a person allows emotion to move with grace, never going cathartic or losing her presence but delving into her inner wisdom, being real, genuine, authentic, and vulnerable. The ego stays in check, not reacting or becoming defensive or taking over. Instead, the emotion rises as the person, centered and aware, observes the self and makes conscious choices. That is power.

To have emotional awareness and agility means to allow the rising of emotions and the sensations that accompany them. It means to be centered in the physical body and containing the rising energy. It means to stay within one's own core hub and gather the information that is being expressed through the rising emotion and to take action, from a fully conscious, body-centered, emotionally integrated, rational mind-oriented state of being. This level of centeredness, when combined with an open heart, supports the expression of one's personal power.

To avoid one's emotions is to decrease one's power because of the amount of energy expended to continually pack those emotions down, trying to prevent anyone, including oneself, from knowing that they exist. The amount of fear and energy necessary to keep the lid on the emotions becomes more taxing than if the person were simply to engage with and listen to the emotion, paying particular attention to the logic or message behind it. Moreover, the alienation from one's inner compass of life (emotions) and the lack of integration of the wisdom behind the emotions leads a person to make important life decisions primarily from her head or ego, losing her alignment, connection to self and source, and her heart. During my years in bodywork, Life

Coaching, and equine work, I have noticed that most humans have at least one emotion they would rather avoid or not feel.

Horses, on the other hand, allow emotion and energy to be part of their life experience. They process the information and decide what they need to do with it. The energy of emotion is a form of communication; the tuned-in nature of their being utilizes all of the information in the environment so they can not only remain safe but also thrive. Once horses process the energy of emotion as information, they return to the healthy state of grazing, resisting nothing and being fully present and in the flow.

Your Thoughts Speak Louder than Your Words

The third key basic component of how horses teach is that they naturally reflect the thinking process or thoughts a human is experiencing. Our thoughts, both conscious and unconscious, create a state of being in our bodies, and the power of being heart-centered. Since horses are finely tuned to the intentions, energy (or emotion), and thoughts that a person holds, they can reflect back the human's state of being and offer opportunity for learning. Horses respond to what you are thinking as much as what you are feeling.

When I lived in Boulder, I had the honor to ride a big and beautiful Hanoverian-Paint cross mare with a big attitude. She was sorrel and white and probably more horse than I should have been fooling around with, but there I was. When I rode her in the arena, Sunshine, a jumper, eyed the jumps in the center. She tried to sneak toward the middle. She was a powerful horse with a mind of her own but completely tuned into the rider's mind. I would giggle when she would eye the jump and then remind her to stay with me, to go slower for me.

One day she and I were trotting around the arena and about to come down the long straight side. I decided to cross the ring on the diagonal. We began to approach the opposite end of the arena. (Remember, at this time I was not fully proficient in my riding skills, but I enjoyed fooling around.) As we cut across the arena, my thought process went as follows: Go left, no, go right, no, go left. Why I was so indecisive and lacking in focus, I don't know. How did Sunshine respond to my thoughts? You got it—she started to go left, then suddenly shifted toward the right, and then even more suddenly shifted back to the left.

I bounced to the left, bounced to the right, and then lost my seat when she took her final left, half falling off while pulling her to stop, all in the span of two seconds. My physical body would not keep up with my active mind, but Sunshine had no problem keeping up with it. It was an important lesson for me to learn the power of my focus and thoughts and how those thoughts affected the horse with whom I was partnered.

Several times while working with clients, I have witnessed a similar pattern when a person's thoughts created their experience. The client engages with the horse while standing on the ground, in any way that they wish. They may sense the horse's energy fields, reach out to physically connect, ask the horse to join up and take a walk around the round pen, or simply stand and reflect on whatever comes to them while in the company of their companion. A woman at one workshop experienced the power of her thoughts, both the positive and the negative, or limiting, thoughts. Once she had completed her body and emotional awareness process, she then established an intention to have the horse come to her so she could experience what it was like to not have to work hard to make things happen (male energy) and to instead allow the flow, trust the process, and receive (female energy). She moved to the center of the round pen and faced the horse. The horse continued to stand along the edge of the round pen, offering only a glance her way when she first entered the pen.

After several minutes of watching the two beings standing silently, I asked the woman what she was experiencing; a vague, open-ended coaching question based in curiosity that always seemed to elicit more information than a specific question would. She said she was waiting for the horse to approach her. I asked her what she was thinking while she waited. She replied that she was worried that he was not going to, that doubtful thoughts were running through her mind, and she was already considering what she was going to do if he did not approach. I asked her how those thoughts were working for her; how were they creating her experience? With a quick light laugh and slight slide of breath, she said, "I get it. This is what I do all the time. I want to receive and I spend all my time worrying that it won't happen, and then it doesn't." Her thoughts were speaking louder than her words.

I coached her through the process of fully identifying the voices that were creating the experience she did not want and the corresponding feeling state she was holding in her body as she thought those feelings. Then we shifted to talk about what she did want. She focused on positive, affirming thoughts that supported her desire and how those thoughts created a different feeling state within her. She identified that she needed to start to think and believe that, "Yes, this horse is going to come to me."

The horse watched our exchange. The client then moved to the center of the round pen and continued with her process, sharing these new thoughts that invited the horse to her. She also focused on bringing her new belief into her heart with her breath. Ten rather long seconds later, the horse turned from the edge of the fence and walked directly to her. He stood by her side and offered his kinship. And the client got it. In that instant, for the first time she experienced what it took to set an intention, clear away thoughts of doubt, hold the feeling of openness, trust the process, and wait for the results to *come to her.* It was the first time she had ever experienced receiving without having to try, by focusing on and *shifting* and *aligning* her feelings (from stress to relaxation) and thoughts (from limitations to possibilities) to what she did want to experience.

When a person reaches this state of true alignment, when thoughts, feelings, and subconscious aspects are aligned with desire and vision, energy naturally flows forward toward that vision; doors open up, and opportunities present themselves. Great athletes will tell you that they achieve great levels of physical accomplishment because every aspect of their being is engaged with not only the possibility of it happening, but the belief that it will. Every aspect of their being and their in-the-moment experience is focused on the same result. They reach a high level of clarity and flow. The heights in my abilities as a skier came only through aligning all of me on all levels so that I was able to become better and better. As soon as I lost my focus, I lost my line, and I lost my balance. Every great horse trainer also has this capacity and understands how their intentions, thoughts, feelings, and actions either create flow and connection or create separation and division.

The importance of this alignment plays out when my clients begin to move from the more reflective and self-aware processes and into more active work with the horse. In the active work, the client, still on the ground, is invited to ask a horse for movement, to maintain movement, and then to transition the horse into and out of different gaits. I help the clients achieve this success by being aware of four things:

1. The position of their body in relationship to the horse

2. The energy (conscious and unconscious emotion) they are holding in their body

3. How they use energy (breath) to assist in increasing the movement or decreasing the movement

4. The thoughts (conscious and unconscious) that they are thinking as they work with the horse

Through the process of actively working with the horse, the clients experience the visceral power of being aligned and creating with another, different living being. They become empowered, centered, engaged, and filled with a sense of achievement. When they struggle to reach these levels of success with their horse, one or more areas of the four points listed above are not aligning with their goal or intention. Once the gap is recognized and the client realigns into all levels of awareness, the horse moves and connects with much greater levels of ease and enjoyment.

The actions we take are always a composite of our emotional and mental capacities and state of consciousness and our connection to our God, the Divine, or spirit. Right action or inspired action comes from a level of awareness in knowing the source of the action. When my actions are taken simply to fill gaps in my life, to feel that I am accomplishing something, to fill a need or to satisfy my ego, they often come up short and flat in energy. It is wasted time. When my actions are in alignment with who I am—my spiritual essence and expression, my feeling and thoughts—they build a powerful momentum for success, manifestation, and co-creation. There is a sense of purpose and connection. Without purpose and without connection, what would life be for?

Afterword

Find Your Passion

The more I align my life to express my core values, the more synchronistic the events in my life become. When I outgrew my life as a ski bum and moved into positions of being of service, opportunities effortlessly came to me. My massage practice helped people become healthy in their physical and emotional bodies. My current life-coaching and equine-learning programs help clients fully integrate aspects of their minds, emotions, and spirits to allow them to listen to their inner wisdom and live a life based in their passions.

Every time my life comes into closer alignment with my values, I let go of various activities, communities, and friends, since we no longer share the same priorities or focus. When I release what is no longer a true fit, I make room for new experiences and relationships. These transitions simultaneously hold sadness and joy.

Achieving alignment means refining where I put focus, intention, time, and, ultimately, action. The more I evolve, the more change I experience. Change is constant. My personal success in creating the life I want is instrumental in my being a good coach for others.

The cornerstone of any success is a person's ability to believe that he or she is worthy, deserving, capable, and willing to create what brings joy. It is imperative for me to look closely at my beliefs about myself, as these beliefs enhance or diminish my ability to live my life purpose.

The more I grow and change, shift my beliefs, align my actions, and live a life based on what makes me happy—being with animals and helping people—the more things unfold with less effort. Ultimately, I was and am already the person I seek to be. I simply needed to find my way back to my true self in order for my authentic self to emerge in the world.

I will be forever grateful of all of the humans and horses that helped along the path of returning to myself. The process of becoming a Life Coach and coaching others to live their passion and purpose is highly rewarding. I encourage you to recognize your natural talents, along with what fulfills you and gives you joy. Find a coach (both human and horse) to help you realize your dreams and bring your gift out into the world for others to receive.

The Horses

My deepest gratitude and continual inspiration come from the connection I experience with nature, animals, and especially horses. All of the horses mentioned in this book, and many more unmentioned, have touched my heart and soul. Through knowing their nature and being with them, I experience joy, love, and passion. Watching horses run free lifts my spirit, and their endless ability to partner with humans expands my heart. There is much wisdom to learn from their unconditional way of being.

Most of the stories in the book occurred over the past seven years. As I wrote each story, I either sought to discover or serendipitously discovered the whereabouts of almost all of the horses involved.

Dragged

The memory of the trauma of being dragged has greatly diminished in my consciousness. This is the only situation where I have not sought to locate the teacher or the horse that I experienced the accident with.

Polo Ponies

The polo ponies live in the same place and are still playing polo. They have a good life.

Hope

Marty Humphreys, my first editor, was so touched by this story that she and her husband offered to drive to Oregon and get Hope for me. I tracked Hope down and discovered that she had developed a condition in her eye that required special care. Luckily the woman who adopted her was a vet technician. Hope is well cared for, grazing in green pastures, and the current owner has no intentions of ever selling her. It gives me a great sense of completion to know that Hope is in good hands. Hope is now around eighteen years old.

Amigo

Amigo, who is twenty-five years old, continues to live at the Epona Equestrian Center and teaches humans in Equine Facilitated Learning programs.

Fly

Fly and Connie are still riding together in the fields and woods near Calgary.

Stone

The young woman who rode Stone experienced some unfortunate events in her life. Stone was sold and then sold a few more times. The last I heard, he was not looking as strong, healthy, or happy as when I worked with him. His potential has not been realized.

Flash

Flash continues to live a healthy and happy life in Arizona, with few or no demands from humans. The neighborhood children occasionally groom and love her, and she gives them pony rides.

Pearl

Last summer a woman in one of my programs began to talk about her horses. As I listened to her, I became certain that I had met her before. Then it suddenly clicked. Shortly after she mentioned her horse Bailey, I said, "And your other horse is named Pearl, right?" Her mouth dropped open. At first she was confused that I would know her horse's name, then was shocked when she realized who I was. Our meeting was so brief years before that neither one of us remembered each other's name. She was thrilled to hear that a story about Pearl would be included in the book. She and Pearl continue to develop a deep bond as she rides Pearl on mountain trails in Steamboat, Colorado.

Hannah Lei

Hannah Lei continues to rest in peace. Two years after her death, I had the privilege of viewing her tail and mane that were saved before her burial. The tail and mane were mounted and framed in her honor. The glorious sorrel color lives on.

Come Together

Cajun lives down the road from my horses. I see him often and admire his magnificent strength, confidence, and intelligence. He explores the mountains of Colorado with his owner during the summer months. In the winter he works at a handicapped riding center, carrying disabled children on his back. He is twenty-three years old.

The Fullness of Moon

Moon continues to be the main teacher in my equine-based learning programs. When we are not working, we ride through the fields and trails of Colorado. His soul continues to be deep and generous. He now looks after Corazon, my mustang, like a grandfather. Moon is sixteen years old.

Lay Down by My Side

Reggie is a twenty-two-year-old Appendix Quarter Horse. Before becoming a therapy horse, Reggie learned how to support a rider who had multiple sclerosis. He holds an American Quarter Horse Association world championship in Hunter Under Saddle and earned another AQHA championship in Pleasure Driving. Reggie was also a dressage horse, showing training and first level, as well as performing in many dressage exhibitions set to music. Reggie, who gives and seldom asks in return, continues to serve as a teacher for humans at the Medicine Horse Program in Boulder, Colorado. He and Connie continue to see each other often.

The Call to Leadership

Patrick is a beautiful eighteen-year-old Thoroughbred gelding. He used to be a registered racehorse. He is used in many programs because of his powerful, yet compassionate, demeanor.

Beau is a ten-year-old Thoroughbred-Paint gelding owned by Karolyn Gazella. He has been with the Medicine Horse Program in Boulder, Colorado the longest of any of the horses. His favorite activity is herd behavior because it allows him to mix things up.

Gypsy is a twenty-one-year-old Morgan horse who used to be a show horse. She is highly respected by the other horses in the herd and continues to capture the hearts, minds, and souls of kids and adults.

All three horses continue to teach humans at the Medicine Horse Program.

The Rebel

Corazon almost left this world in the summer of 2008 because of colic. However, his strong resolve to stay and many invaluable events that I believe were guided by a higher being kept him here on Earth. He has much to learn and continually shows me how his trust in me and Moon has grown. Corazon taught his first group of students in 2008.

Like a Horse

Sunshine was pregnant when I worked with her. One day while I groomed her, the word "Moonshine" popped into my mind twice. I offered this name to the owners to give the newborn baby. Later, after I have moved to Tucson, I heard that Sunshine had given birth to a healthy black and white Paint named Moonshine.

Becoming an Equine Facilitated Learning Professional

As the benefits of working with horses become more understood and experienced, the field of Equine Facilitated Learning is rapidly expanding. If you have a passion for animals and for helping people, you may be attracted to explore this work. The stories shared in this book demonstrate the variety of ways and the depth of transformation that many people experience when working with horses. Equine-based learning programs are complex due to the emotion and energy shared and exchanged by both human and horse. It is a newly emerging field that needs to be honored and respected.

I highly recommend that individuals who are interested in this line of work enroll in a training program to learn the nuances of the work and how to keep clients, horses, and yourself safe and healthy. These skills cannot be achieved through a few days of training or by reading a book. To facilitate sessions requires horse skills and human communication skills (coaching, therapy, counseling), along with knowledge of aspects of mind/body integration, healing, and leadership. In addition, you must learn how to properly prepare people for their experience and support them in integrating their learning back into their everyday life.

Finding an EFL Expert to Work With

After reading this book you might have discovered a desire to participate in an equine-based learning experience. Like any other professional service, research your potential facilitator and learn about his or her background. Consider the following questions when researching facilitators or programs:

- How much horse experience do they have?
- What professional skills do they offer to support your experience?
- With whom did they study to become a facilitator?
- What is the focus of the program offered?
- How long have they been offering this work?

For more information about EFL, programs, and resources, please visit my Web site at: www.CoachingwithHorses.com.

References

Beck, Martha. *Finding Your Own North Star: Claiming the Life You Were Meant to Live,* Crown Publishers, 2001.

Budiansky, Stephen. *The Nature of Horses: Exploring Equine Evolution, Intelligence, and Behavior,* The Free Press, 1997.

Budiansky, Stephen. *The World According to Horses: How They Run, See and Think,* Henry Holt and Company, LLC, 2000.

Coats, Margrit. *Horses Talking,* Rider Books, 2006.

Gendlin, Ph.D., Eugene. *Focusing,* Bantam Books, 1981.

Goleman, Daniel. *Emotional Intelligence: Why it can matter more than IQ,* Bantam Books, 1995.

Judith, Anodea. *Eastern Body Western Mind: Psychology and the Chakra System as a Path to the Self,* Celestial Arts Publishing, 1996.

Kohanov, Linda. *Tao of Equus: A Woman's Journey of Healing and Transformation through the Way of the Horse,* New World Library, 2001.

Kohanov, Linda. *Riding Between the Worlds: Expanding Our Potential Through the Way of the Horse,* New World Library, 2003.

Levine, Peter. *Waking the Tiger: Healing Trauma,* North Atlantic Books, 1997.

Lowen, Alexandra, M.D., *Bioenergetics,* Penguin Books Ltd., 1975.

McElroy, Susan Chernak. *Animals as Guides for the Soul,* The Ballantine Publishing Group, 1998.

McLaren, Karla. *Emotional Genius,* Laughing Tree Press, 2001.

Oriah Mountain Dreamer. *The Invitation,* HarperSanFransisco, 1999.

Pearce, Joseph Chilton. *The Biology of Transcendence: A Blueprint of the Human Spirit,* Park Street Press, 2002.

Pike, Kathy. *Pathways to a Radiant Self, A Journey of Growth and Discovery with the Chakras,* PTR Publishing, 2002.

Raschid, Mark. *A Good Horse is Never A Bad Color,* Johnson Publishing, 1995.

Resnick, Carolyn. *Naked Liberty*, Amigo Publications, 2005.

Ruis, Don Miquel. *The Four Agreements: A Practical Guide to Personal Freedom, A Toltec Wisdom Book*, Amber-Allen Publishing, 2001.

Swift, Sally. *Centered Riding,* St. Martin's Press, 1985.

Williamson, Marianne. *A Return to Love: Reflections on the Principles of "A Course in Miracles",* Harper Paperbacks, 1996.